KIN

*DECADES OF SURVIVING THE
EVOLVING FAMILY DYNAMIC*

Kin \'kin\ n [ME, fr. OE cynn; akin to OHG chunni race, L genus birth, race, kind, Gk genos, L gignere to beget, Gk gignesthai to be born] (bef. 12c) **1** : a group of persons of common ancestry : CLAN **2 a** : one's relatives : KINDRED **b** : KINSMAN <he wasn't any ~ to you –Jean Stafford> **3** archaic : KIN-SHIP

We are all KIN;
We are all FAMILY.

[signature]

KIN

DECADES OF SURVIVING THE EVOLVING FAMILY DYNAMIC

by

Rex Paul Martin

Cover art by Tom Decker
Book design by J. Michael Albrecht

DISCLAIMER

THE CHARACTERS AND PERSONALITIES DESCRIBED IN THIS BOOK ARE PURELY FICTIONAL. ANY SIMILARITIES OR RESEMBLANCES TO PERSONS LIVING NOW OR WHO ARE DEAD ARE PURELY COINCIDENTAL. DESCRIPTIONS OF PERSONALITIES AND EPISODES OR SITUATIONS INVOLVING THEM HAVE BEEN FABRICATED BY THE AUTHOR FOR THE PURPOSES OF THE THEMES OF THIS BOOK

DEDICATION

More than anyone in the world, I love my Sam. He has been my soul partner and teacher for almost 40 years. He is the kindest, most unconditionally forgiving and intelligent person I have ever known. He has accepted me through unimaginable insults. I dedicate this book to you, Sam. You, more than most, understand the dynamics of family culture. Thank you for making our family what it is. It is what it is.

I lovesya!

ACKNOWLEDGMENTS

Mahalo to Ann Mills, my patient and sensitive editor. Many thanks to Mike Albrecht, my technical Guru. Kudos to Tom Decker for his artistic contributions on the cover design. A lifetime of gratitude and admiration to the spirits who have been my teachers and guides: my bio-family, my friends, my special loves and my animals.

Thanks to my gang: Em and Brad, Ann, Sue, Nancy and Steve.

To Ricardo and Kyle – you have no idea!!

Mostly, to the one, Sam, thank you.

Thank you all for being my FAMILY.

CONTENTS

CONTENTS

PREFACE
THE CHALLENGE OF FAMILY

The structure of the American family has been changing so rapidly over time that anyone exploring understanding traditional or alternative families faces a frustrating task. No matter what our cultural, religious or ethnic backgrounds may be, wrapping our minds around the evolving concepts of family requires patience and a life-long dedication to acceptance and resignation. Just when we may have settled in to a comfortable niche of the definition of family, along comes a new and startling complication. Traditional family is perplexed by emotional and economic realities: divorce, single parents, teenage pregnancy and unwed mothers and fathers, same-sex marriage, and adoption. Alternative families have formed, spawned by the feminist movement, stay-at-home dads, and communal life style choices. Terms are confusing: nuclear family, extended family, married partners vs. unwed partners, cohabitation, breadwinners, and gender roles. Movies and television have opened our eyes and hearts to endless forms of relationships that are now considered family entertainment. Where is it all going?

The percentage of married-couples with children under 18 has declined to 23.5 percent of all households in 2000 from 25.6 percent in 1990 and from 45 percent in 1960. The percentage of single-parent households has doubled in the last three decades, but that percentage has tripled between 1990 and 1950. According to the U.S. Bureau of Census, since the

1940s, the marriage rate has decreased while rates of divorce have increased. The number of heterosexual unmarried couples has increased tenfold, from about 0.4 million in 1960 to more than five million in 2005. If same-sex partners were included in this statistic, it would increase by at least 594,000. One in nine of all unmarried couples are gay men or lesbians.

Critical to the current nature of the American family is the changing role of women in households. Women working within the house today are not the same as those 50 years ago as they continue to pursue careers and become bread-winners. The amount of time all women spend doing house-work, regardless if their partners help out, declined from 27 hours per week in 1965 to less than 16 hours in 1995. According to the *New York Times*, in 2001, wives earned more than their spouses in almost a third of married households where the wife worked. According to the US Census Bureau, stay-at-home dads are not as popular as they are in Europe or elsewhere in the world, nevertheless there are an estimated 105,000 stay-at-home dads who are married fathers with children under 15. These dads do not work outside the home, while their wives bring home the paychecks. These dads care for 189,000 children nationwide.

It isn't only the adults who are changing the profile of families. Children are forcing family life to adapt as they face pressures and expectations from all sides. About 50,000 children were adopted from foster care in 2001. Fewer of these adoptees were older children, with the average age being 7 years old. Gay and lesbian partners are choosing to raise children, either biologically or through adoption. In all couples studied, 66 percent of female same-sex couples and 44 percent of male same-sex couples live with children under 18 years old. In the 2000 census, there were 594,000 households that claimed to be headed by same-sex couples, with 72 percent of those having children. Children are a significant presence in single-parent homes as well. The presence of children living in single-parent homes has increased from 4 percent in 1960 to 42 percent in 2001. Mother-child families make up 83 percent of these households.

Our homes are flooded with the portrayal of the changing American family in television and movies. We have grown accustomed to more honest reflections of our lives in shows such as "The Cosby Show," "Married with Children," "All In the Family," "The Jefferson's" and "Good Times". Alternative family life has also been exposed in shows such as "Half & Half," "One on One," and "Murphy Brown". Further out in more recent times, we see thought-provoking views in "Sex and the City," "Two and a Half Men," and "Glee".

****

The individuals and families that you will meet in this book come to life on these pages because I need to share them with you, and I believe that you will want to know them. While the names and factual circumstances of these characterizations have been fabricated, my hope is that you will meet, in them, people familiar to you in your own life. My goal is to liberate your identification with these characters and their stories through humor and education. If you find yourself persuaded toward one concept or another, you may want to discuss your feelings with other members of your family. You may feel relieved or unburdened from baggage that you have carried since childhood. Mostly, I hope this book will touch your heart and help you to define or re-define your family experiences.

All of the people who have come in and out of my life as inspirations for this book are deeply loved and will always be cherished as my teachers and mentors. I forgive them, as much as I ask their forgiveness. I offer them my integrity while I recognize theirs. Along the way, we must laugh and learn. Whether we like it or not, we will always be family. We are all KIN.

KIN

*Decades of Surviving the Evolving
Family Dynamic*

THE ONE

I believe in love at first sight. I believe in dreams that come true and the end of the rainbow. I believe in wishes made on falling stars, blowing out birthday candles and pennies tossed in fountains. I give kisses for luck and keep dried shamrocks... all because of Joel.

The first time I ever saw Joel, the first time I watched him walk across campus, the first moment he looked me in the eyes, the first words he spoke to me, and the moment he took my hand, I was in love with him. I couldn't breathe; nothing else in the whole world mattered, except him.

Feeling helpless is not in my nature. I do not give over or give up. But, when I met Joel, I lost all powers to think clearly, see a way out, or care more about anything or anyone else. All I wanted was to be everything to him. He had become everything to me. He became more important to me than anyone before I met him. And, there has never been anyone since who has been more important to me than Joel.

When you spend more time living with someone than you were alive before you ever met him, you are transformed, and you lose all perspective. After thirty-six years of life with Joel, I laugh at the banter about being co-dependent. Well, of course we are co-dependent. Who wouldn't be? Psychologist types talk about that as though it were a bad thing. I suppose if you are in a relationship with someone for a brief amount of time, say two years or so, and you are co-dependent, then, hell yeah! Get into therapy if it bothers you. But, when you get to the point where you finish each other's sentences and know what the other person is going to say before he even open his mouth, then get over it; learn to live with it. It is a blessing, not a curse.

Honestly, when I hear or read about these couples that have been together for 30 or 40 years and then split up, I am absolutely convinced that one or both of them have completely lost it. Oh, I know, I know....somebody found themselves, or somebody just read a book about "It's Never Too Late to...(fill in the blank)". To me, it would be the same feeling one would have if a partner had died. You would grieve and feel that loss for the rest of your life. Why would you consciously choose to do that? How could you honestly tell yourself after all that time that you don't love that person anymore? When you have defined yourself in the context of being part of a relationship for several decades, how do you meaningfully redefine that definition of self?

This does not at all mean that I adore every aspect of Joel's personal habits or traits. After all these years, we are nothing if we are not honest with each other. Besides, after 36 years, you cannot hide your true feelings. We both wear our reactions like comfortable old clothes. We are predictable and familiar in each others' skins. We have learned when to make a big deal out of something, and when to just let something go. We have become masters at timing, waiting for just the right moment to suggest buying a new dining room table or replacing a car. On a smaller scale, Joel tends to be overly dramatic and I am often understated. So, we do a lot of reading between the lines and interpreting.

Back in 1974, on the campus of the University of Washington, Joel was a senior working on his under graduate degree and I was returning to graduate school after working as a teacher for 3 years. He was 21; I was just turning 26. Because I spent about 8 hours a day doing research in the graduate library, where Joel worked, I had my eye on him every time I passed through his check out turnstile at the exit doors. In those days, pre-terrorist fears and high-tech security, students had to submit their backpacks for inspection when leaving the library in order to make sure that no one was stealing books. Just so that I could get closer to Joel, I would enter and leave the library more times than necessary when he was on duty. Too shy to actually speak to him, we came within inches of each other for several months without saying a word.

Most of my classes were in the evening. One Wednesday night, class was cancelled. The Gay Students Association meetings were on Wednesday nights, but because of the conflict with my class, I had never been able to attend. So, this particular evening I saw an opportunity, and headed over to the Commons building to slip quietly in without being noticed. As I entered the room, just like in a gay bar, all eyes turned to see who the new guy was. Embarrassed, I looked to the front to see who was speaking. It was Joel. He was the President of the organization. After the meeting, he made a bee-line for me, we introduced, and he asked if he could walk me back to my dorm. The rest of the beginning of our story happened very quickly.

My birthday was a week later and I asked Joel if he would like to go to a dance concert with me to celebrate. After the show, we stopped at a Dunkin' Donuts and sat in the glaring lights getting to know each other. We discovered our mutual love of chocolate and ate far too many sinful donuts in our nervous anticipation of the future. A few days later, I came back to my dorm room to find a card and a candle waiting for me: "I hope we get to use this sometime: Happy Birthday, Joel".

In the next month we actually drew up a list of all the reasons why we should and should not move in together. Of course, the positives outranked the negatives, and we soon found our first apartment. We paid a whopping $90.00 a month. The view out the window across the parking lot was the Bonney Watson Funeral Sign and clock. We figured we would always know the time. That apartment building on Nagle Place is gone, as is the funeral home and the clock. A few years back, Joel brought me a brick from the demolition. It is now a subway station in a trendy park.

We decided to combine our honeymoon with a tour I was leading through Europe in the following summer of 1975. For two months we trundled around England, Holland, France, Germany, Italy and Spain with 4 other college students, one of whom was my brother, Nino. We were a crazy lot, out for a lark and horny as hell. There was one woman in our group. She held her own quite nicely among us 5 gay guys. Suzy was voluptuous and available in every town we stayed. Before the trip, she had bought a dress and a pair of non-sensible shoes at Nordstrom's. She wore the hell out of that outfit for the two months that we camped and moved about. At the end of the trip, she had the gall to bring the dress and shoes back to Nordstrom's and claim that they were defective. Characteristic of that grand store, she got her money back. Now, that took huevos!

Traveling together is an ardent test of a relationship. We passed. That fall, we settled in to the next phase of our life together: finishing grad school, finding first jobs, setting up a real household for a tentative new family. Joel decided to go to law school, and, as if we didn't have enough on our plates, we started the first cautious conversations about adopting. It took 5 years to make that happen. In the meantime, we experienced all the joys and tears that young couple's experience. The trauma and ecstasy further deepened our love for one another.

In 1978, still living life at break-neck speed, we moved in to the first apartment building to be completed in the renovation of The Pike Place Market and we started our business downstairs – THE PIKE PLACE MARKET CREAMERY. Those were wild times. I would teach during the day and come home to close down the Creamery, which Joel had worked all day. He would head off to Law School for night classes, and I would clean up and do the day's receipts. On weekends, I would run the shop, Joel would study and we would clean and restock together on Sunday and then start it all over again the next day. We foolishly did our own quarterly taxes in those days, to save money. Once every three months, we locked ourselves away in a motel somewhere, and, after tearing our hair out, did not emerge till the job was done. This produced more laughter and tears and established a pattern of teamwork that serves us well to this day.

Owning and operating THE CREAMERY was mostly good fun. Everyone in Seattle comes to The Pike Place Market and it is a required experience for tourists. When we lived and worked there, it was closed on Sundays. Now, it is open every day of the week. Those of us who lived there looked forward to Sunday as a day to kick back and take a break from being nice to tourists. We loved the locals and looked forward to our favorites: local TV personalities, like Jean Enerson, Charlie Royer - then mayor of Seattle, Emmet Watson – newspaper columnist, and even Julia Child would shop in our Creamery when she was in town to do a cooking demo. We carried a heart-stopping 49% butterfat cream, which Julia Child could not resist. We could not resist it either. Late at night, when Joel came home from law school classes, we wandered downstairs into the shop and gathered up cream, and chocolate ice cream to make the best late night snack in the world. Years later, we were still trying to shed those sinful pounds.

The Market was rife with characters and personalities. One regular was named "Just Happen to Have It", which is what he said every single time we told him what his bill was. Another older guy we called "Keep An Eye Out" as he peered at us with his one eye, the other side hidden behind a patch.

There was Edith, the bag lady, pushing around her grocery cart, cursing the airplanes as they noised across the sky. Most of the customers were polite and fun, but one fellow always stole butter from us, after buying something else as a decoy. We carried duck and goose eggs and one summer I hatched them out in an incubator on the counter top, timed just right for a busy Saturday before Easter.

Eventually, our dreams of adopting finally came true and we could no longer live in our small apartment above The Creamery. We did welcome our first adopted son into our family at that apartment while our new home was being readied in another part of the city. Even today, he refers to the place as "…that hotel where we stayed in downtown Seattle." Shortly after that, we sold The Creamery, bought 10 acres and built a house in the Skykomish Valley on the highway to Stevens Pass. We called the place "Greyrose" and lived there off and on for 20 years. It was magic.

Greyrose was a fantasy world that we created in a wide, wet valley about an hour northeast of Seattle. Deep into the woods, far back from the road, we were surrounded by fairy rings of old growth cedar trees, maples, hemlock and alder. On a daily basis we encountered countless deer, coyotes, flying squirrels, eagles, pileated wood peckers, and the occasional bear. Our "A Frame" house was heated with two wood burning stoves. One stove was an old fashioned cook stove in which we made amazing meals and heated water. For the first ten years there, we had no electricity, no phone, no indoor plumbing or toilet. We created an outhouse in an ancient spruce stump that had been cut about 8 feet up from the ground. The center of the stump had rotted out. All we had to do was build steps and a roof, mount a toilet seat, and then sit there surveying our forest kingdom that lay at our feet.

Off to the left of the front deck we installed a cedar, wood burning hot tub, with a submergible cast aluminum stove and pipe, guarded from the bathers by a cedar wood fence barrier. It took about three hours to heat the water to a desired temperature, but when it was ready, there was nothing more heavenly than to soak in the tub, in the middle of the woods, in total silence staring at the stars above or feeling snowflakes hit your face. Sometimes we would have guests and often, as many as 6 of us would be enjoying the tub when a herd of deer would surround the cabin and stare at us strange human creatures who had invaded their turf.

Walking up the road to the cabin one day, we looked up into the blue sky and saw an eagle flying toward us with a huge salmon in its talons. Just as it was straight overhead, it dropped the salmon at our feet. Feeling blessed and in awe, once again, of the Greyrose magic, we sought out an Indian Shaman to ask what the significance of that event had meant. He looked at us and smiled and said, "It means you're damn lucky"!

Over twenty years of life at Greyrose, we held retreats for as many as 25 guests, family gatherings, memorial services, birthdays and holidays and even enjoyed being snowed in or flooded in depending on the season of the year. We grew sprawling gardens with so many fruits and vegetables we had to give away our excess. My father's ashes are scattered there, as well as many of our friends' ashes, mostly those who had died of AIDS.

The day we packed our final things up after selling Greyrose to the county's FEMA operation was one of the saddest experiences in our life together. Joel and I sat on the steps and cried and held each other, incredulous that our decades' journey through this Middle Earth was at an end. All good things do come to an end, but most of the time they are replaced with better, or at least equally amazing experiences.

There are so many, many other stories that crowd more than 36 years of life with Joel. They certainly have more than filled and enriched my life. At this point, I feel I must be the luckiest man in the world. Being in this relationship, making this family, is the hardest work I have ever done. It is also the most rewarding.

FIRST FAMILY

I am the oldest of six children in a Catholic-Italian family. Being first in the line-up of siblings, I know where all the skeletons are buried. My handsome father, Casey, was a traveling salesman. He had girl friends in every small town on his routes. Bella, our mother, was the only child of Italian immigrants. She loved and hated my father, while worshipping her own father. Casey was home three nights a week. He obviously did his duty on the home front fathering six kids, but he was busy otherwise. I remember the scene one night when Bella came sobbing into my bedroom with a love note that she had found in one of Casey's suit pockets. It was from some gal in another town. We were going to leave him, so I needed to pack things and be ready to move. Huh? I was in the second grade.

One Saturday afternoon, when I was twelve, Bella went into labor with my youngest sister, Ultima. Bella lay on my other sister's bed and moaned and cursed Casey. She ordered me to get on my bike and ride to the local tavern to pull Casey from his bar stool, where he had been keeping vigil all day.

Years later, just before Casey died of heart failure at 58, in 1983, he grabbed me by the shirt and said, "Take care of your mother for me!" Throughout the ensuing funeral arrangements, services, receptions and cremation, I was a rock. Walking in a trance, I tended to Bella, delivered a eulogy, smiled and greeted guests and relatives and, only in the privacy of my own bedroom, did I allow myself to cry. My sister,

Cara, said at the time, "How are you doing this? You are being so strong."

Devilla, the second after me in the family, has been estranged from all of us for years. Dev married the wealthy son of a wealthy banker. Her husband, himself, was the president of a bank and Dev had no more use for Bella's cloying emotionalism – Casey used to say that she could cry at basketball games. Dev also had no interest in the petulant whining of her three sister-rivals. She was a little more tolerant of my brother and me, only because we were more distant and didn't demand anything of her, in the way sisters can do. Dev was happy, finally, with her Cadillac and her big house with a view. Bella would try to patch things up by sending Dev's two daughters expensive gifts. Dev would send back a note to Bella informing her that she had sent the gifts promptly to the Goodwill, and please, don't bother her anymore. So, 1983, when Casey died, was the last time anyone heard from Dev. I made a few inquiries over the years to ask her the cause of her silence. I only received more silence. I speculated that Dev had been scarred early on by Bella's relentless criticism and shaming judgment, inferring she was a slut and stupid and wouldn't amount to much. I guess Dev's goal was to show her, and then be done with us.

After a while, like that pair of old shoes at the bottom of your closet, unless you discover them again one day, you forget you have them. Nearly 30 years later, unless I run across a fading photograph of Dev or some memento that Bella still displays from our childhood, I forget I had her as a sister. I can no longer conjure up any feelings for her – no sadness, no disappointment or regret. I don't even wonder what she looks like now. Even Bella has let her go, as if she had never given birth or raised her.

On the other hand, this estrangement from his sister, Devilla, was very difficult for my brother, Nino. Nino is a twin to one of my sisters, Ragazza. He is, as most middle children, tortured with keeping the peace and smoothing out the problems. Being dutiful and conflicted with a desire to achieve and be successful like his mother wants him to be, he is equally drawn to settling for the least common denominator: no worries, don't push the river and don't make waves. Nino lives a tidy little life, in a barren, sterile environment – no children, no memberships or commitments to clubs or organizations, no highs, no lows, just keep it clean and organized and everything will be all right.

When he was growing up, Nino never missed an episode of "The Donna Reed Show". He often asked our mother, Bella, to be like Donna Reed and yantz around the house in a dress, high heels and an apron. I would come home from school and find her sitting in the living room, dressed up like that, smoking a Pall Mall, unfiltered, and reading the paper. "How was school today, dear?" I could never answer that question except to say, "Fine". First of all, she didn't really want an answer. And, secondly, she really wanted to ask my brother, not me, because he was the one in the fantasy.

Nino recently broke his finger scrubbing his kitchen sink. That was after he had washed his car, again, for the second time that day. I'm sure that he and his partner own stock in Costco. Their garage is insulated from floor to ceiling with endless rolls of paper towels, cleanser, antibiotic sprays, bleach and sanitary wipes. They don't go outside much – there's dirt out there – and if they ever have to do some disgusting project like cleaning out flower beds or sweeping the deck, those clothes go immediately into the wash or, better yet, in the garbage. They have long since stopped eating at pot lucks or sleeping in hotels or motels. They don't travel for that reason. I'm quite surprised they still eat at restaurants, although I am sure they bring those sanitary wipes to autoclave the silverware and drinking glasses.

There is a dark tether between Nino and me, two gay men, only brothers in a family dominated by sisters. Bella tells me he "looks up to you". I don't believe it. I think he resents me and resents his placement in the lineage. The older we get, the more he condescends to me and lectures me about what a dead-beat son I am to his mother. There is something big that is missing in Nino's life. He tries to fill the space up by assuming the role of the 'man' of the family. He calls family meetings. These are like faculty meetings that he is used to attending in his job as a teacher. He takes charge, assigning everyone tasks and writing notes, which he promptly sends out on email afterwards. He spends an inordinate amount of time fawning over Bella. Of course she loves that. He takes her to breakfast and always includes her in his parties – she, the only female among the gay crush of adoring, good look-ing men.

Nino avoids spending any time alone with me. He is afraid he will most certainly have to be the 'little brother'. I don't care about that. He has worked so hard to build the persona of Bella's protector, the family guy, the go-to man. I just wish he would let me tell him that I love him and that the roles are unnecessary.

Nino's twin sister, Ragazza, was also the recipient of Bella's acid tongue: "We will be lucky to have some man take Ra-gazza off our hands". To fulfill this prophecy, Ragazza came within 5 credits of graduating from college in her senior year, and abruptly withdrew to get married. A talented artist, she has never been able to shake off Bella's conclusions about who she is and what she needs to do with her life. Perhaps more than any of the rest of us, Ragazza was irreparably dam-aged by constant programming from Bella that she was weak and needed a man to take care of her. When Ragazza does assert herself and act independently, she receives clucking disapproval from Bella: "Your husband is so good to you. He doesn't drink or carouse around. What do you want? What else could you ask for? You have everything. What are you going to do if you leave him? Where will you go"?

Ragazza is sweet and generous to a fault. We call her bio-daughter 'Barbie'. She has everything. Unlike her adopted Chinese older siblings, 'Barbie' doesn't do ….house work, dishes, laundry, her hair, yard work or cooking. Ragazza fixes her an entirely different meal from the rest of their family and even cuts her meat for her, still. The 'girl' is 20. I love Ragazza and wish that she could calm herself into knowing that she is capable and valuable. We need to have lunch, alone, some day, and cry and laugh and forgive.

The second to the youngest sister is Saint Cara. After multiple marriages (we call her the 'Liz Taylor' of the family) she spends every moment of her life caring for Bella and her own children and grandchildren. She juggles a busy professional career – never mind the aneurism and the double knee replacements. If Cara isn't taking Bella shopping, cleaning her bathroom – Nino will come in later that day and clean it again, just because – taking her to the doctor, buying groceries for her own children and grandchildren, flying around the entire western United States for her job, and cooking for her helpless boyfriend, she is attending her best friend who is dying of leukemia, organizing the Special Olympics or phoning me to tell me how much she loves me. I'm exhausted just thinking about how she gives of herself.

Cara did not escape Bella's wrath either. I remember when we were all little kids; it was Christmas. I was about twelve and Ultima, the youngest and last child, had just been born. Cara came down with some mysterious illness that landed her in the hospital. Bella was certain it was meningitis; it wasn't. Cara was five. I was walking through the crowded living room, holding new-born Ultima, and tripped over a hassock and fell on the floor with the baby. Bella swooped over and snatched the infant from my protective arms and hissed, "If you have hurt her, I will never forgive you". When Cara got home from the hospital, having recovered from whatever had afflicted her, Bella proclaimed that she was weak and damaged and there couldn't be much we could ever expect from her. She has spent the rest of her life proving Bella wrong.

Saint Cara has struggled with her weight, the men in her life, and deflecting Bella's disapproval for over fifty years. She is one of the strongest, most capable and resilient people I know. She has always respected my chosen family. Despite the withering bombast from Bella about everything she is and does, Cara is loyal and hard working to support her. Cara will always have my utmost respect.

Possibly the most neglected and hurting of all the siblings in the family is my youngest sister, Ultima. Ultima is now in her fifties; no longer the blond, skinny, life of the party. She walked away from the family and all responsibility for anyone and anything many, many years ago. She lives isolated and care-free in a large city far away from the rest of the first family. She is angry, conservative-Republican, pro-gun, pro-Rush Limbaugh, anti-gay, paranoid and struggles, as most of us in this bio-family, with long standing abuse issues.

She decided some time ago that she wasn't a lesbian after all. The alcoholic, chronically unemployed boyfriend, with whom she now lives, likes her so much that he let her buy a condo for them. She supports him as long as they can party and dream about owning a winery someday.

It isn't easy keeping track of six children. Inevitably, you lose one here or there. On a Sunday afternoon in 1964, Casey and Bella packed up what they thought was the whole fam-damnly into the Chevy Caprice station wagon, and headed over to Bella's parents' house for the obligatory Sunday dinner. We were at Grandma and Grandpa's house for quite some time before someone noticed that Ultima was missing. Casey and I scrambled into the car and headed back home; Bella remained back, hysterical, to finish eating her mother's lemon meringue pie.

When we rounded the corner of our block, there was Ultima, standing on the sidewalk, crying, lost and abandoned. She has been that way ever since.

Ultima is disassociated, dispassionate and unconnected. She has refused to financially contribute anything to Bella's up-keep. She states that it is the duty of the welfare system to pick her mother's bloody head up off the floor when she falls and that she should be in a nursing home supported by social security. More than Nino, Ultima is vitriolic against me, her oldest brother. I am accused of being an intellectual, a do-gooder, a snob, and a fag.

When Ultima and her lesbian lover, Tobie, drove out West to spend a vacation with Joel and me, in 1980, she was a dope-smoking, hard-living, liberal feminist. Now, her boyfriend won't allow her to have a computer in the house, receive any mail with bar-coded address labels, or watch Oprah on TV because he is sure that 'they' are spying on them.

18

The middle children, Nino and Ragazza, defend Ultima, excusing her and covering for her inanity. When Ultima comes to visit her mother, Nino and Ragazza roll out the red carpet and pretend that she isn't crazy.

I mourn the loss of Ultima's communication and her affection. She is truly hurt. I do not know how to heal her wounds or how to soothe her pain. I am not a magician or wizard. She does not and never will trust me. I wish her well and hope that someday she will be at peace.

I am grateful to this cast of characters and to all the other members of my bio-family. They have been my teachers and guides in this present incarnation. I believe I chose them to learn what I needed to learn about surviving the evolving family dynamic.

FAMILIES AND HOUSEHOLDS – A CHANGING DEMOGRAPHIC

"Relations are simply a tedious pack of people, who haven't got the remotest knowledge of how to live, nor the smallest instinct about when to die." - Oscar Wilde

When I was growing up in the 50s and 60s, divorce was a taboo topic akin to cancer, mental illness, pregnancy outside of marriage and homosexuality. Everyone I was allowed to associate with came from a respectable family – dad, mom and kids living in homes with grandparents nearby. From the outside of these homes, all seemed normal. You went to school and church, joined scouting and sports teams and didn't embarrass the other members of the family. Once I started making my own choices and associations, I learned that what happened on the inside of these homes did not always match what seemed apparent on the outside.

The U. S. Census Bureau's *Report on Families and Households* published in November, 2010, reveals some notable changes since my childhood.

Men and women are waiting longer to marry. The median age at first marriage increased to 28.2 for men and 26.1 for women in 2010, an increase from 26.8 and 25.1 in 2000. This increase is a continuation of a long-term trend that has been noted since the mid-1950s. In addition, the overall percentage of adults who were married declined to 54.1 percent in 2010 from 57.3 percent in 2000.

According to *America's Families and Living Arrangements: 2010*, the average household size declined to 2.59 in 2010, from 2.62 people in 2000. This is partly because of the increase in one-person households, which rose from 25 percent in 2000 to 27 percent in 2010, more than double the percentage in 1960 (13 percent).

Even though the overall household size declined between 2000 and 2010, some household subgroups increased in size. For example, households where the householder had less than a high school degree increased to an average of 2.87 people in 2010 from 2.67 in 2001.

Other Highlights:

- The percentage of households headed by a married couple who had children under 18 living with them declined to 21 percent in 2010, down from 24 percent in 2000.

- The percentage of children under 18 living with two married parents declined to 66 percent in 2010, down from 69 percent in 2000.

- In 2010, 23 percent of married couple family groups with children under 15 had a stay-at-home mother, up from 21 percent in 2000. In 2007, before the recession, stay-at-home mothers were found in 24 percent of married couple family groups with children fewer than 15.

- The percentage of children under 18 who lived in a household that included a grandparent increased from 8 percent in 2001 to 10 percent in 2010. Of the 7.5 million children who lived with a grandparent in 2010, 22 percent did not have a parent present in the household.

Last November, the daily local newspaper carried the usual "Dear Abby" column. This particular issue was on family dynamics. The first letter was written by a wife who was advising a previous letter-writer to divorce her husband because he refused invitations to events from her family. She said he was anti-social, even though he loved his wife, because he did not want to participate in '…normal family functions that are so important in bringing people together.' This letter-writer had divorced her second husband because he was like this man, and family meant too much to her.

A second letter-writer, this time a man, claims he has not gone to family functions with his wife since 1995, and, in his opinion, it has worked out just fine. No matter what he did, talk too much or too little, spoke too loudly or couldn't be heard, mixed too much or not enough – he would get chewed out by his wife. In his words, his wife was so socially insecure, no matter how he acted, she took issue. I would like to hear her side of the story.

The third letter, which struck a note in my heart, was written by a woman who grew up in a large, boisterous, affectionate Italian-Catholic family. Her husband grew up an only child in a conservative home. Her family gatherings so overwhelmed him that he could only attend one or two per year. She attended the rest alone. They had heated arguments about his dislike of her family until her mother became ill and he watched how they all came together for her care. According to her, that is when he came to know and appreciate her family on a different level. I would like to hear his side of the story.

Victor Borge said, "Santa Claus has the right idea. Visit people once a year."

Why do we put up with demoralizing and demented atrocities leveled at us by family members when in any other venue, we would be calling 911? In my case, the answer is clear: most abuse happens to children at the hands of their parents. The term 'abuse' is relative. Yes, there is physical and sexual abuse, perhaps the most notable kind. But there is also a kind of abuse that leaves invisible scars. Unlike cuts and scratches that benefit from a good scrub and bandages or fresh air, psychological scars fester in the dark, often unattainable regions. Mercifully, even memory cannot sometimes find them. If it is possible to retrieve these events and haul them to the surface, exposing them to the light, they can sometimes begin to heal. The therapy is in the telling.

Taking naps always seemed like a boring waste of time to me. Even as a 5 year old. Not understanding that it was my mother's way of taking a time-out, I used naps to enjoy play making. I can't remember if my sister had been born, or if I was still the only child. Every afternoon Bella would put me in my room, close the door, and not come back to get me for what seemed like an eternity. We did not have television yet, so any dramatic idealizations that danced in my head must have come from books, or my complicit grandmother. She didn't mind that I would put on her bathrobe or drape myself in her biggest lace table cloth. At her house, I could flame around, trailing my robe, pretending to be the queen (not the king) holding audience for all my subjects. It was more fun if I could climb up on the ledge next to the stairwell and let the lace drape far down the wall for the full effect.

Back at my house, with my bedroom door shut for nap time, I must have sensed that this was something that a five year old boy should not do. With all my puny mite, I pushed the dresser in front of the door, for security. It also provided the perfect 'throne' on which to perch with my bedspread cascading to the floor, as I spoke to the imaginary crowds.

One afternoon, I must have been speaking too loudly. Abruptly, Bella pushed at the door, trying to get in. I was not strong enough or quick enough to stop her entering the room, discovering me in my gown and a sweater flounced over my head for flowing locks of royal hair. Even now, the look of disgust and disbelief on her face is burned into my mind. I had never been so afraid of anyone. What happened next happened fast. Before I realized what she was doing, this person who I thought was my protector, called all the boys in the neighborhood to sit on our back porch steps. She forced me into a chair at the top of the stairs, in one of her most feminine dresses, with lipstick smeared across my mouth. She locked the back door so that I could not get in. I could not escape. A dozen boys, some older than me, blocked my way down the stairs. The door was locked. I had no choice than to sit there, crying, while these playmates of mine laughed, jeered, cat-called and mocked me. Bella watched from the kitchen window.

After that, I didn't want to be around other boys. Bella's approval was illusive, Casey encouraged her; nothing I ever did was good enough, or manly enough. At five years old, I knew I could never count on them to protect me or accept me. As a five year old, all I had was me and I would never be able to depend on my parents to take care of me. My first family was not a safe place to be.

POISON

Two toxic tools of manipulation in my first family are guilt and shame. These helpings of poison were liberally doled out by my mother as often as she could get them down our throats. Italian mothers are similar to Jewish mothers; there is essentially no difference between their use of language or tears. They both get their way using guilt and shame. Guilt and shame are human weapons. When family members use these, it is for the purpose of dominance and control. They are tools born from deep fear and distrust.

For example, I remember being lined up in the kitchen when we were all too young to defend ourselves. Bella would have a huge bottle of cod liver oil in one hand and a giant spoon in the other. Each one of us had to take a ghastly, greasy, stinky spoonful of that nasty goop because "Its good for you. What? You want to get sick? I work hard all day around here and you can't take a little something that will keep me from having to break my back taking care of sick children? That is the thanks I get? You're just like your father. No appreciation for what I do. You don't love me."

Casey converted to Catholicism in order to marry Bella. My grandfather was horrified that his only child was marrying this blond German guy from a big city who had no education and was fresh out of the service. The fact that he wasn't Catholic just added insult to injury. My grandmother thought Casey was handsome and was charmed that he liked her cooking.

So, my grandfather and the priest guilted Casey into conversion in order to be accepted into the family.

There was never any question that I would go to Catholic schools. For some reason, I did not attend kindergarten. Rather, I trotted off to first grade when I was five years old, sweltering in the warm September air in corduroy, wool sweater and khaki long sleeve shirt – the parochial school uniform.

In the first grade, and for every year after that, the priest would come into the classroom and we would all bolt to attention, standing beside our desks. He would ask, "How many girls are going to be nuns?" All the girls would raise their hands. "How many boys are going to be priests?" All the boys would raise their hands. Years later, in 8th grade, I was one of only a couple boys and girls who were still raising their hands. Bella would remind me of this expectation, loudly and in public, as often as she could. "Rexy is going to be a priest, aren't you, Rexy?" It wasn't long before my friends began to taunt me with a new nickname: "Sexy Rexy."

"Rexy" did end up going into a monastery after high school to study for the priesthood. Three years later, I was out on the streets again, changing the course of the history that had been destined for me since first grade.

VAMPIRES

Everyone has a family. Even if the people we call family are not blood related. Even if forced on us at some point, everyone finds themselves in a family. Somewhere between birth and death, if only momentarily and accidentally, we are part of a family. And, once part of that family, for as brief a period as it might be, we are forever a member of that family. Like not being a virgin, even if you only had sex once and never again, you will forever not be a virgin. Wishing family away does not work. Even if all the other members of the family die, except you, you are still stained, indelibly, with that family.

My partner, Joel, and I have two adopted sons who are part of our family. Early on, in making them family, we learned that they still considered themselves part of their original birth families. Both sons had not seen their mothers in years, and both had never even met their bio-fathers. Yet these two boys, very different from each other in almost every way, ache to be part of their bio-family. They were relieved to be part of the family that Joel and I created with them. Both were happy as an adopted person can be to have a place called home and grown-ups to call parents. But, both boys never stop hoping that someday, somehow they will return to what nature originally had planned.

Putting together an adopted family, as in the case of adopting children legally, is never what the adoption agencies portray it to be. It does not matter how rich or well educated you are, nothing can guarantee that, at some point, the adopted children will not make your life a living hell. This is not in the same way that bio-children will make their parents suffer. At some point, adopted children break their parents' hearts. They have to. Nature, not nurture, wins out. If an adopted child is ever going to make sense of their life, they have to find out where they came from and why that is missing. This dictates turning away from their adoptive parents, even for a short while. Adoptive parents need to be told that this is going to happen eventually, and prepare them, as best they can, for this inevitability.

Intentional families, i.e. those created by an act of choice or resignation, are built with love or necessity. By default, these families are extensions, like the way starfish can grow another arm. Strangers who find themselves with other strangers in a new family will never have the same experience as bio-related individuals. That is why the bond between fathers and children or mothers and children will always be more compelling than the bond between the non-blood related two individuals (the 'mother' and the 'father') who created them. Thus, divorce between two parents is easier than blood related individuals walking away from each other.

Having said all this still does not mitigate my feelings that my bio-family bugs the hell out of me! I feel like the tar baby. The more I grapple with reconciling the experience of growing up in my bio-family, the more painful it becomes. I want to come to peaceful terms with their existence. Peace eludes me. Every day that I do not phone my mother only means that tomorrow I will once again have to decide if I am going to phone her or not. Every time my righteous younger brother attacks me for being a dead-beat son, I want to tell him to go to hell, but I don't. It wouldn't do any good. It would only confirm his opinion that I am ungrateful, disrespectful, and a creep. He learned how to use guilt and shame quite expertly from his mother.

So, what does one do to avoid suffocating in the closet of family expectations?

I have observed many people who have been hurt, even damaged irrevocably, by family members. While I consider the existence of a family like a classroom or a garden where things grow or perish, I do not want to give the impression that I condemn any individual family member who acts from learned, or, what some might even consider, instinctual motivations. One common characteristic of elders or leaders in families is that they strongly believe that what they do is in the best interest of the family. An example of this is the relentless indoctrination of children into a particular religious belief system. Some see this as natural and appropriate; others have termed this as child abuse.

I know a man whose parents made him kneel down in front of the bible and a lit candle when he was three years old. They told him that if he did not accept Jesus as his personal savior, he would go to hell. This man was smart, even as a three year old; he recognized these adults were bigger and more powerful than he, and decided, at that time, to capitulate. Of course, the scars of that incident are with him to this day.

What children do to others in the family constellation is part of the growth of learning, as cruel and senseless as it may appear from the outside. Children, in our society, are not held responsible for actions that they will be accountable for later in life when they understand legal, adult expectations. For adults to shun children and condemn them as 'spoiled', 'lazy', and 'worthless' is only a reflection of the inability of that adult to be effective with that child. Not all adults are talented and skillful at effective child rearing. It would be best, in families, if these adults were counseled not to spawn children or to be near them in their development. Of course, that is a description of an ideal family situation.

A recent *New York Times* article discussed how young Americans were becoming increasingly diverse. The result is that white children have become the minority in ten key states, including Arizona, where racial tensions are heated. The article proceeds to ask the question whether older whites will be willing to educate a younger generation that looks less like their own white children than ever. And, how will the diverse younger generation feel about caring for the needs of aging whites? Again, Arizona families lead the discussion with 42 percent of its young people being white, compared with 83 percent of its residents being white and sixty-five or older. Last year's census estimates report that, of the twenty-four states that gained children in the last decade, whites contributed to the growth in just eight. The highest was Utah, where their share was 43 percent.

In Virginia, a largely suburban state, the population of white children was in decline. In contrast, the number of mixed race children doubled with Asian children up by more than two-thirds. According to Kenneth M. Johnson, a demographer at the University of New Hampshire, "Living in the suburbs used to mean white family, two kids, a TV, a garage and a dog. Now suburbia is a microcosm of America. It's multiethnic and multiracial. It tells you where America is going."

It is common for siblings to blame and hold grudges against one another for hurtful actions that took place while growing up in the family. The stressors on children in diverse family groups, searching for their place in the rapidly changing American landscape, can be hurtful. I am not only talking here about ethnic or cultural diversity, but sexual diversity, economic, intellectual and physical diversity as well. While it is unfortunate that painful experiences may occur, it is more debilitating to hang on to these feelings and to let them color adult interactions for the rest of your life. People change and grow. The chrysalis produces beauty and enlightenment.

Some of us spend our entire adult life working hard to re-play the tape burned into our brains from our adult family members. We strain to re-direct and re-formulate patterns of learned behavior. My partner and I have observed in our two adopted sons indelible habits, belief systems, and responses to new learning and reactions to other adults that were etched into their consciousness in early childhood. Our first adopted son came to us when he was eight years old. He lives with Asperger's Syndrome. As a form of autism, children who live with Asperger's respond from a view of the outside world that is like static on the radio: when the signal is coming in clear, they can understand and be understood. When the signal is not clear, who knows what is coming in or the meaning of what is coming out? Our other adopted son came to us when he was thirteen. Both boys had lived in as many as twenty foster homes before being adopted. It is an understatement to say that they are scarred and disabled in more ways than any psychological labels can apply. In the end, the best we could do for them was to provide an environment, for as long as they were with us, that gave them stability and consistent identity – something that they never experienced in their prior lives with other families. Our challenge is to accept them as they are without judgment or disapproval.

Many of us, who come from families where we have been judged and not accepted, escape as soon as possible. Some of us run away, some cut off all contact with the abusive family members, and some tragically choose suicide as the answer to the pain of family rejection. The present climate of bullying that we are experiencing in the world today is not limited to peer groups. Many children and even adults experience bullying from family members, mostly older than they. Sometimes, unlike bullying from outside family sources, the type of bullying occurring inside families is subtle and masked as caring or instructive. Family members who feel bullied by other family members must be very clear with themselves, often with the help of trained professionals, to determine how they truly feel about the way they are being treated.

We cannot very often or very effectively change other individuals, especially if they are older than we are, such as elders or leaders in our families. So, my advice to those who feel never ending guilt and shame coming from another family member, or, the entire family structure, is to get out as fast as possible. We will never change them. They don't want to change. They want us to become their clone. In the words of a friend of mine, "…unfuck yourself"!

One more important thought: When we first start the extrication process of walking away from an abusive family, it feels awful, and the tendency is to blame ourselves. Don't! My brother tries to guilt and shame me all the time by telling me that my feelings of guilt and shame are created by myself and that he is not responsible for that and only I can do that to myself. While in deep, deep psycho-babble that sounds valid, I reject that line of reasoning. Remember what I said earlier. Those family members are experts at using guilt and shame to get us to conform to their expectations of how we will behave as a member of the family. They will inject us with their personalized serum and will never relent until we do what they want out of guilt and shame. When we first start shaking off the guilt and shame hangover, we may report feeling terrible, (i.e. guilty and shameful), for rejecting the family. That is exactly what they want us to feel. We have been inoculated. At that point they follow up by turning on the heat: phone calls, emails, letters, or, the opposite – they shun us and ignore our attempts to make sense of things with them. We are in their stupor. They will not capitulate. They will not be satisfied until, like vampires, they have infected us with their virus and we finally become one of them.

FAMILY RECIPES

Formulas are essential to survival. No matter how angry or rebellious one may become, unless we submit at some point to the exact ingredients formulated toward a particular ending, there will be no successful outcome. Substitutions rarely work. The expectation for conformity and consistency is strong in families. Some families have rigid expectations that the children will go to college; others just want us to get married, have lots of kids and live next door. Religious families require church attendance at least once a week. Catholic families hope for a priest or a nun to emerge. Mormon families need missionary youth. Poor families acquire 'stuff' to buffer themselves from the pain of indignity. Hispanic families need food and babies. Jewish families need other Jews. Gay families need to be proud and resolute and included. And each particular flavor of 'family' may not necessarily agree with the ingredients that make up the other families.

There is one commonality that all families seem to share. No matter if we are rich or poor, Christian, Muslim, Jewish, or Atheist, Democrat or Republican, American or European, Asian, Black, Native American....whatever ingredients formulate our family, we must never, ever defect from the family. Defectors will be shunned. Defectors will be judged. They will be bullied, if not into submission, at least into silence. Some of those who question FAMILY VALUES will even be hounded to their deaths. They will not be tolerated by the family elders, siblings or offspring.

Escapees from family night and family meals, family bowling tournaments, obligatory baptisms, first communions and confirmation ceremonies, birthday parties, bar mitzvahs, weddings and funerals often run away, and seek other immigrants journeying in an alternative world. They attempt to establish a parallel universe where Sundays are liberated from church and spaghetti dinners. They get unlisted phone numbers and do not send Christmas cards. They go on solitary vacations. They buy themselves gifts for their birthdays and spend New Year's Eve watching "Harold and Maude" for the 5th time.

Viewed as ingrates, they will be pursued. Family will hunt them down for an apology and, hopefully, a conversion. They will be lured, bribed, and tricked back to the family at any cost. Guilt and shame will flog them back to the nest, bosom, homestead, traditions, rituals, ancestors, shields, code of arms, and money.

Nothing obligates and cements family members together more than birth and death. New babies are an integral part of the recipe. On the other end of the spectrum, grieving the death of one of the family unlocks forgiveness and bonds the members together in an irrational embrace.

Irrationality seems to be another essential in the family formula. The hippies become rabid Republican Tea-baggers. Agnostics and atheists become born-again Christians. Pot smokers become evangelical health fanatics. Sermonizing, moralizing bores become addicted to pornography and alcohol. The ones that stay the same live into their 90's and die peacefully in their sleep. But, no matter what, if they played by the rules, they are still bona fide, card-carrying members of THE FAMILY.

In my own bio-family there are heroes, heroines and villains. Some of the certified members of the family would consider me to be a villain – one of the defectors. In my mind, my Italian Grandma will always be my favorite heroine.

JIMMINY CRICKET

My little Italian Grandma's name was Alma. Most people called her Gigi, and some called her by her irreverent nickname, Niera, "Blackie". She was darker than most Northern Italians, thus the reference to Blackie. Even when she was in her 80's and had lost her leg, she still insisted on dying her hair jet black and, with a ruler, drawing her black eyebrows in a line across her forehead. When she was dying in that stinky nursing home, I didn't recognize her at first: hair combed back revealing gray, no eyebrows or her signature red lipstick. She looked childlike in that bed, angry and withdrawn, comatose, but still hearing everything that was said about her. I sat next to her, telling her what a wonderful Grandma she had been to me, thanking her for all those $20 dollar bills she had pulled out of her bra to give me, her first and favorite grandchild. I saw a tear roll down her cheek and I knew she could hear me. Feisty to the end, she yanked her head to one side when I tried to give her a sip of water. She never liked water, hardly ever drank it. What was I thinking? I didn't know until a few hours later that I was the last one of our family to see her before she died. Bella, out of fear and frustration, had ordered her out of the hospital and into this wretched nursing home where she died a few hours after arriving. Bella had seen her into the bed, but was driven out by the incessant screams of the person sharing the room with Grandma. On the other side of a thin curtain was a longtime resident, obviously atrophied and arrested in development. The only thing 'she' could do was to screech and scream out her misery.

This, and the smell of rancid urine, was the environment my dear, sweet Grandmother had to endure in her final moments. Bella had made sure that her favorite, my Grandfather, Uomo, died in an antiseptic private room in a hospital. Bella was their only child. She adored her father and battled with her mother. She never really made peace with Gigi, and never talked about her decision to place her in the nursing home.

My Grandmother made an art out of housecleaning. Someone said you could eat off her floors, they were so clean. I never saw a speck of dust or anything out of place in her house. But, she never made you feel beholden or uncomfortable. She was all about making you feel welcome and at ease. In grade school, a big treat for me was a day when I could leave the school at lunchtime and walk the two blocks to Grandma's house where she had fixed a huge, hot lunch: two kinds of meat, pasta, vegetables, French bread, salad, and, for dessert, her famous homemade lemon meringue pie. It was just me and Grandma sitting at the table, she watching me eat with great satisfaction and me encouraging her to tell stories of the old country. I don't remember her ever eating the lunch – just serving me and enjoying my enjoyment.

There were so many Easter dinners and Christmas feasts and just plain old Sunday afternoons with Grandma working all day making homemade pasta or roasting something Italian. I never saw her wear trousers, always dresses. Most of the time, if she left the house, she wore high heels. She was classy. And, unknown to most, she was the real strength and backbone behind my Grandfather – a realization that was lost on my mother. Bella idolized her father. He was perfect in her eyes. No man, least of all her husband, Casey, could ever measure up to Uomo's sainthood. To this day, she walks around with his cane and sleeps in the antique bed that was his for many years. She takes on more and more of his imperious mannerisms. She never mentions my Grandma. Grandma's birthday was last week. She would have been 106. But, a day doesn't go by without Bella mentioning some moony, sentimental memory of her father.

Like many people, I have made choices that I regretted. Afterwards, we ask ourselves, "What were we thinking? It sounded like a good idea at the time." Asking Bella to move into the rental house we owned next door was one of those bad ideas. She was in her 80's. She had wasted all the money that her father had left her. She lost her home and her car and could not be left unattended. The old guilt and shame mantra kicked in and I stepped forward as the oldest son to fulfill my promise to Casey. After all, my siblings had been caring for her every weekend for years. I was semi-retired now. Joel and I could do this. I mean, what could it take? The answer to that became EVERYTHING: our time, our money, our peace of mind and damn near our relationship with each other and our sons.

Feeling dutiful and righteous, we moved mom in next door and suddenly we were on call, 24/7. We became her nurse, cook, social worker, whipping boys, and all manner of roles that we never expected to come with that much proximity. My brother, Nino, came out to visit once a month. He would show up at my house, fortify himself with a drink in order to go over and see her. Of course, he would fulfill his OCD fantasies cleaning her toilet and sinks. Then, an hour later he would show up at my house again for a nap or another drink. After a total of two or three hours, he would say his goodbyes till next month. My sisters, Cara and Ragazza, were not into cleaning, but it was pretty much the same routine except they would bring pre-cooked food for her freezer, which Bella refused to eat. I would look into the freezer periodically and throw it all out; they would start over again, pleased that she liked their food so much.

So it was that Bella became more and more dependent and less willing to be left alone. She started taking on the personality of her father, using phrases he would repeat, launching into sermons that I had heard him deliver to me when I was a little boy. That was when she started walking around with his old cane that she had somehow acquired from the stuff that he had left behind.

Grandpa's old cane broke and Bella asked me to try to fix it. I tried. It was irreparable and dangerous to continue using. I gave it back to her and said that maybe she could just keep it as a souvenir remembrance. A few weeks later, my sister arrived for a visit. She handed Bella Grandpa's old cane, glued and patched together by her husband, my brother in law, a "real" man. Bella grinned and never said a word to me about it. Her behavior was so much like my grandfather: devious, tricky, selfish, and greedy.

My grandma was just the opposite of all that. She always put others first. She saved the best for everyone else and took what was left over for her. Her happiness was seeing others happy. Grandma had a funny expression – more odd than many of her broken Italian utterances. When she was amazed or surprised at something, she would exclaim, "Jimminy Cricket!" (I think this was a polite way of avoiding saying "Jesus Christ!") It came out like "Geemany Crrrreekeet" To this day, my sisters and brother and I mimic some of those fond old expressions of hers: "Dao u au" – "There you are" and "Seesors" – "Scissors". She had lots of Italian words also, some of which will forever remain mysteries. When she felt sorry for a little boy, it was "Porett", and for a little girl, it was "Poretta". "Lazaron!" was what she called good-for-nothing people – mostly men. And, of course, there was the ever popular slur for women she had no use for: "Beech!"

On Mother's Day, 2006, the year Bella moved in to our rental, the whole family gathered next door at Bella's to pay homage. She was the enthroned Queen, seated on the front porch, her adoring children fetching her food and bringing gifts. She cooked nothing, offered nothing, and was first, not last –her father, Uomo reincarnated in a pant suit, banging her cane for attention. She poked and waved the cane at her great grandchildren because she could, because she deserved the deference, because it was her turn, and her time.

I sat off in the distance and out of the corner of my eye I could have sworn I saw a little figure, spry and neat as a pin, bustling about preparing the next dish, arranging the table, washing a pot, serving, serving, and I thought I heard her say, "Jimminy Cricket! What can I get you? Mangia! Mangia!"

A few days later, Bella said to me, "You don't like those family get-togethers any more, do you?" I said, "Oh, it's not that...it's just that something is missing. It's just not the same." Bella replied, "I don't know what you mean." I said, "Yeah....I know. Never mind. Can I get you anything, mom?"

SUNDAYS WERE HELL

"Now I lay me down to sleep and pray the Lord my soul to keep. And if I die before I wake, I pray the Lord my soul to take. God bless mommy and daddy and my brother and sisters. Amen." – Anonymous

Every night, growing up as a little boy in my first family, I would kneel beside my bed under Bella's inescapable eye, and say my prayers. In our family, we prayed before dinner, on special occasions, and before bed. Sunday, we all piled in the car to go to Mass. Casey would come with us sometimes, but, more often than not, he would stay home, which would be the beginning of a fight between my parents that would last all day. Sundays were hell. After Mass, we would come home and run for our rooms to distract ourselves with books or pretend games. If we pretended enough, we would not hear the yelling and crying in the other rooms. Sometimes I would pray then. "Please, dear God, stop them from fighting." As if God was listening, occasionally there would be a lull for a while.

When the fight ended, we would pile in to the car again and drive to my grandparents' home for Sunday dinner. Casey drank beer. Bella stuffed down her emotions with Grandma's wonderful cooking. We all finished the afternoon with homemade lemon meringue pie while watching Disneyland on one of the first color TV sets in the neighborhood. Those were the days when you had to manually adjust the color.

Still, the images on the screen were garishly red or Kelly green. This constant jumping up to adjust the color would start another fight, this time between Casey and Grandpa. That, in turn, would cause Bella to side with her father, her idol. We all were then whisked into the car; the ride home and the rest of the evening would end with more fighting.

I suppose some might consider these episodes as family bonding. I saw them as all the more reason why I had to get out of there as soon as I could plan an escape. An opportunity arose at the end of the 8th grade. I asked to go to an all-boys seminary in Oregon. Casey and Bella wouldn't go for it. Four years later, at seventeen, I managed to find the most radical jettison possible: a contemplative, cloistered monastery in northern California. In one sense, it was a trade of one dysfunctional family for another. But, at least in the monastery, I didn't have to talk to the other members much, and my bio-family could only see me once a year.

A MONK AT 17 IN A NEW FAMILY

Making choices for all the wrong reasons seems to be my hallmark. No one could have had a more romantic delusion of religious life than me, the young Brother Paul of the Holy Family. This was the name I took at the beginning of my novitiate year. The irony of choosing that name is not lost on me now.

In the late summer of 1966, at the height of the Hippie movement, Bella and Casey and all but my youngest sister piled into the Chevy Caprice station wagon and drove me to the monastery in northern California. I had been accepted as a novice into a contemplative, cloistered Discalced Carmelite Catholic Order of Priests and Brothers. At seventeen, I was one of the youngest to enter their order.

Before delivering me to my new family, we stayed a couple of days in San Francisco, just south of the Napa Valley where I would be living. My father was extremely uncomfortable in crowds, a self-conscious man who was somewhat embarrassed trouping his large family around like the Trapp Family Singers on tour. Bella loved the spectacle. She even sewed identical dresses for herself and all the girls, with matching hats and cosmetic cases covered in the same fabric as the dresses. She made Casey and my brother and I wear identical shirts and trousers. We looked ridiculous.

To draw even further attention to this traveling gypsy group, Bella would talk to complete strangers about who we were, where we were from and why we were there. At one point, after a meal in Alioto's restaurant on Fisherman's Warf, my sister Cara threw up out on the sidewalk, all over herself and anyone else within projectile distance. Bella and the girls all burst into tears, Casey and I had to run for paper towels to clean it all up, and Nino asked if this meant that we would not be going to Madam Tussaud's Wax Museum. Gratefully, that was the end of having to wear the matching outfits, since they were now ruined. Later that week, I exchanged my matching outfits for the matching brown robes worn by all the other members of my new family.

In the dark, silent cloister, I thrilled at the fasting, the vegetarian lifestyle and the self-denial. Every night when I climbed into my board bed, sans-mattress, perched on two sawhorses, I said a version of "Now I lay me down to sleep…" in Latin. I found getting up at 2AM to chant for an hour, then back to bed and up again at 5AM for more hours of chanting, Mass, and then silent prayer – all electrifying! Beating myself with The Discipline – a cat of nine tails dipped in wax, I would beg for my food at meals.

The monastery family, while purporting to be ethereal and mystical, was more like a hen-house or a bee-hive. Everyone had a job to do; there was definitely a pecking order. Most noticeably, there was a hierarchy, and I was at the bottom of the heap. I was the last to enter, the youngest, the most vulnerable and gullible. Including myself, there were seven 'brothers' as we were called, that entered in my class: Carl, a young man from the deep south, who could never get used to austerity or kneeling for hours at a time. James, a goofy college graduate, was the only one among us who eventually stayed in the Order and made it to the priesthood. Michael, a petite French/Basque chef had a hard time giving up pâté and Beaujolais. Steven, a Mexican-American ex-drummer/musician, ended up drowning in the swimming pool. Dale, a hunky, shy, gay man transferred into the Carmelites from the Christian Brothers to get away from the temptation of his love interest there. And, Thomas, a smart, sassy, funny fellow – the only brother near my age – was the one with whom I promptly fell in love.

These were my seven new brothers in a family of about twenty-five men. All the older priests were from Ireland, sent to California to establish an outpost Province. We lived in the mansion of a former sea captain, high on a hill at the end of a winding road in Napa Valley. The house and grounds gained a sort of fame in the filming of "Gone With the Wind". Two famous scenes were recorded there. There was a series of descending fish ponds, beside which Rhett and Scarlett's daughter breaks her neck and dies from falling off her little pony. The second, and more famous shoot, was made on the staircase that we ascended and descended many times in the day and night. It was where Rhett uttered the cruel line, "Frankly my dear, I don't give a damn."

In addition to being vegetarians, we fasted every day (eating only one meal) from September 14th, the Feast of the Holy Cross, till Easter Sunday. There were no newspapers, magazines or television. We could not receive visitors except once a year. We spent the entire time in silence, except for one hour after the daily meal in the evening. The day was divided between working in the gardens to grow our food, scrubbing and cleaning the house, including that famous staircase, more chanting and silent prayer, and then lights out by 9:00PM.

Wednesday's, between Easter and September 14th, were glorious! It was summer in the Napa Valley, and the seven brothers were allowed to take a long walk for a couple of hours, through the vineyards and orchards. We picked forbidden fruit and gossiped and teased one another. These Wednesday afternoons were some of the best family hours of my seventeen years so far. We all grew close to each other and, even though I have not seen any of those men, except for Philip, in over forty years, their faces, their laughter, even the smell of their sweaty brown robes are etched into my mind and heart. For one memorable year, we were an unforgettable family.

At the end of the Novitiate year, monks profess their vows of poverty, chastity and obedience. It is a very formal occasion, attended by bio-families, and religious dignitaries. We were then shipped off to various other monasteries for study and further training. Even though some of my class of seven came with me to our new family in the foothills of San Jose, we were fractured and grieved the loss of our idyllic hidden nest up north. One by one, we started dropping like flies. Brother Carl left and returned to the Deep South where he married some young woman and worked in a grocery store. James had been sent to Rome where he was eventually ordained a priest. Michael left to return to San Francisco and the restaurant scene. Steven, who couldn't swim, but insisted on exercising in a swimming pool, drowned, lying there for hours before anyone found him. Hunky, shy Dale returned to his parents' home in Colorado, and, last I heard, was living the life of a mountain man, shunning the world, but without brown robes. Thomas left, and came back and finally left for good. He went on to get a doctorate in Theology and Education. He actually lives, not too far from me, with his wife. When we both became public school administrators, we would run into each other at educational conventions. Who would have guessed?

After three years in the monastery, I knew I was conflicted. The realization of my sexuality was emerging, inappropriately confined in the monastic life. I grew more and more interested in literature, poetry, music, playing the guitar and young people in the outside world who were thriving in the liberated times of the early 70's.

When I finally decided to leave, I cried for three days. How could this be happening? What was to become of the little boy who kept raising his hand from first grade on, pledging his dedication to the priesthood? I did not want to return to my first family; I couldn't remain in my second family. Wearing a hair shirt and a chain tightened around my thigh was romantic! But, nature IS stronger than nurture, and, after three years, I knew it was time to stop running. I had not been able to become myself in this family either.

So, still in the pattern of making fateful moves, I found myself on a plane, zooming back to my first family. We have all heard that admonition: you can't go home again. The next two years were a series of more lessons in how to live with the consequences of one's choices. I became engaged to a sweet, unsuspecting young woman, thinking it was the right, and only, thing to do. Finishing college became a chore and a prelude to the rest of my life. Eventually, nature won again; the engagement was off, graduation was behind me and I was smothered in my first long-term relationship with a man. Would my third family bond be the charm?

The answer was a resounding NO! Fast-forward to 2008. By that time I had been with my soul mate, Joel, for twenty-four years. We had two sons by then, thriving careers, and I finally knew that love makes a family. As a member of the local school board, I was sent back to the town in which I grew up to attend an educational conference. I just couldn't seem to escape that town, or the memories of living with my first family there. That visit, I was determined to seal the crypt once and for all. Having no more family there, or friends that I contacted, I wanted to close the door on the past.

A CLEAR CONSCIENCE IS USUALLY
THE SIGN OF A BAD MEMORY

I don't have a clear conscience. My mind is the type that records events in a photographic way. Sometimes the pictures are moving. My heart records sensory experiences – the feel, smell and sound of the good and the bad. There is no delete button in my brain. I cannot seem to backspace or escape. I'm always hitting ENTER, ENTER, ENTER, and then SAVE.

There was a French philosopher who developed a theory of time. Most of the Western culture wants to organize time in a linear progression, past, present and then future. This particular philosopher asked what time would look like if it was all happening at once. Imagine yourself looking into a Plexiglas box, with various levels separated out as you gaze through the box. You can see people and events and history from the first level (the past), the second level (the present), and the third level (the future) all happening at the same time. Thus, there really is no delineation or linear development because all events are simultaneous.

When my ninety-two year old Italian grandfather, Uomo, was dying in his hospital bed, he would wake up out of his attempts to fade away, and tell me things about his life: how to make wine, building his family home in Italy, fishing in his favorite creek, eating my grandmother's good cooking. His life was playing out in his mind. I remember he said, "My life has gone by so fast. All these things seem like they just happened yesterday."

Maybe they did just happen yesterday. Maybe they happened today. Grandpa knew he was passing to the life between lives and he registered amazement that the life he was living had passed by so quickly and was coming to an end. We should all be so lucky to be as calm and reflective as he was. He felt no pain; he was relaxed and comfortable as he looked down through the Plexiglas box.

Surviving growing up in a bio-family is a relief. Being able to live through it, more or less intact, is a memorable accomplishment. All grown up, I look back, down, sideways and beyond. Sometimes I feel like a snake or a crab that has shed its skin or shell. I take a few steps away and look back. There is my old self, and I now have a new self, but all of what is me is there, past, present and the promise of the future, side by side, together. I also know that as I continue to do this shedding process again and again as I age, it will look and feel the same evolution, only the details change.

My parents and siblings are all grown up now. They are grey and wrinkly, as am I. But, in actuality, we are the same people, the same personalities, with all the gifts and faults that we had when we chased each other around the house or played hide and seek in the back yard. When I am having a glass of wine with my sister, the database in my brain shows me feeding her baby food in a high chair, like it was yesterday or this morning. When my brother fires off a wilting email detailing his latest complaint about me, I see him trying to sneak through the house with a banged up knee, leaving a trail of blood from the front door to the bathroom, where he locked himself in, refusing to tell anyone what had happened. Nothing has essentially changed. He's still a mystery.

Some people in families have selective amnesia about past events. I do not revise my memories; I just select those pages out of the photo album that are important or meaningful to me now. The important thing is to use those memories as learning tools, not as weapons or cattle prods. If I have truly internalized a lesson learned from past experiences, the chances of creating more fulfilling or enlightening events in the present or future are greatly increased. Forgiveness and reconciliation are natural outcomes of internalizing the learning. How does the saying go? "There are no mistakes, just lessons to be learned."

Having said that, I am not one to hang around where pain and remorse are being doled out. Recognize it, and move on.

When I reflect on what I have learned about family, I find myself selecting some images that are difficult to look at because of the painful memories they evoke. Some of the images are not as painful as they are embarrassing or humorous. Most of them are poignant reminders of what is or is not important. I am also not one who believes in the popular phrase, "It's all good..." In addition to selecting family memories, it helps me to sort them into understandable categories, like painful, embarrassing or humorous. Some other categories are useful to me, as well: unnecessarily frightening, inevitable, unavoidable and, I hate to admit, regrettable. When I get too deep into memories, and the air starts being sucked out of the room, I then look at some of the faces in the frames and say to them, "I didn't say it was your fault; but I still want to blame you."

Different family members view certain memories differently. Parents often relate stories at family get-togethers that they think humorous, but children may think embarrassing. What may seem poignant to one member of the family, or unavoidable, might be painfully frightening to another.

In 1953, my sister Devilla, snuck into my bedroom in the middle of the night and whacked me on the head with a baseball bat. I was seven, she was three. To this day, when I am down or feeling beat up by the world, I will crawl into bed and pull the covers up all around my head so that only my face is peering out. I lie on my back in order to be prepared for an attack; my internal database of childhood traumas remains intact.

It was also there, while living in that big house on the boulevard in 1953, that a woman was murdered in the alley in back of our house. I was lying in bed on my back, covers in the protective position after the baseball bat attack, when I saw a woman come to my bedroom window, knocking, scratching, clawing at the glass. It was the middle of the night. She said nothing, just frantic to get my attention. My heart was in my throat as I slid over the side of my bed and tore down the hallway to my parents' bedroom. It wasn't easy waking them up, and Casey was not pleased with my hysteria. Of course, when he came to my room, flipped on the light and examined the window, there was no one there. Following a round of "Go back to sleep. You were just dreaming. You have such a wild imagination. You're just like your mother. Now, calm down and go back to sleep", I hid there under the covers, eyes wide, staring at the window for a long, long time.

The next morning, while chasing each other around the house, the door bell rang, and we all peeked around Bella's skirt as she spoke with a man in a suit who flashed a police badge. "Good morning, Ma'am. Did you or anyone in the house hear anything unusual last night? Did you see any scuffling in the alley or hear any cries for help"? "No officer. Nothing like that happened. It was quiet all night. Why"? "Well, Ma'am, a woman was murdered behind your house sometime in the night, and we wondered if you knew anything that could help us." "No, sir, we were all asleep."

After the officer left, Bella shut the door and turned around to see us all standing there. She looked at me, and suddenly, she and I knew exactly what had happened. Could we have prevented this? If Casey had believed me, would that woman still be alive?

When I tell this story at family gatherings, my siblings roll their eyes in condescending disbelief. Bella, of course, does not remember such trivia in thirty years of raising six children. For my part, I still insist on big, loose down comforters and extra pillows and long sheets — all the better for tucking around my face when the lights are out and the world is a mean place, and I remind myself that there is nothing wrong with my memory.

PARENTING YOUR PARENT(S)

Bella later said I looked pale and shocked. We had just arrived at the Post office. I left her at the front desk to buy some stamps and went around the corner to get her mail out of her box. The next thing I knew, I heard screams and commotion. I raced back to the front to see her lying face down on the floor, not moving. "Mom…are you all right?" She was barely conscious. She had tripped on the rug at the front door and hit her head on that obnoxious beeper device that lasers your presence to the workers if they are not at their post.

Gratefully, the personnel called the paramedics, who checked her out and believed her dismissals of their concerns, the fools! I thought to myself: I know this woman. She will suffer publicly for the attention. She's Italian AND Catholic. Of course she doesn't have broken ribs, even though they hurt when she breathes. Of course her knee is O.K., even though it is the same knee that was ruined in the last time she fell in her house a month ago. Of course she doesn't have a concussion…"Where am I? Who are you?", she moaned.

To further play to her audience, she announced to the entire crowd that gathered, "Oh, this is my son. He hates it when I do this. He hates being embarrassed by his mother. Look at him. He's pale. Maybe HE is the one who should go to the hospital." I thought, great. Kick me while you're down.

I stepped up to the counter and asked the two postal workers if they had accident/injury forms. They both shrugged, pointed to each other and mumbled. I gave up, and decided to bag the rest of the excursion with Bella and get her home.

"Mom, please, at least take some Advil." "What for? I'm fine," she said as the bruise began to blossom on her forehead and she limped down the hallway.

A few weeks later, all my siblings and their entourage came out to visit Bella and the plan was to take her out to a brunch, which we had reserved at a local restaurant. At the last minute, Bella decided not to join all of us. Ever the martyr, she made her royal pronouncement: "No, no…you all go and have a good time. I'll just be here by myself. I'll be fine. Don't worry about me. You just all go and enjoy yourselves…" O.K. fine! Several hours later, when we came back to the house, we found her lying on the kitchen floor in a pool of blood, having hit her head on the counter top on the way down from another one of her numerous falls.

It was at this point that Joel and I began an extended discussion about Bella's care and our ability to cope with her medical issues on a daily basis. Both of us were working full time and raising a teen-ager. The rest of the siblings lived 150 miles away. The answer to our questions came soon when Bella fell, again, walking around the garden. She had wedged herself between two stumps and could not get up. Luckily, she was wearing the bracelet, which she hated, allowing her to push a button and call the emergency response company. The company called the nearest relative, which should have been me, to determine the need for care. I was at home next door, going about my business, when I received a phone call from my brother, Nino. "Did you know that Mom is lying in her front yard and that an ambulance and the police are on their way?" he says in a know-it-all tone of voice. "Why are YOU calling me?" I asked. "Well, apparently, I am the one listed on the first-responder list for important family members."

Swallowing my indignation, I headed next door to greet the growing mob of EMT's and police workers. And, of course, Bella launches in to her usual "This is my son; he hates it when I do this..." I followed the ambulance into the city and spent the day at the hospital with her while they took X-Rays and determined the level of injuries. Bella's biggest concern was what they had done with the jewelry that had been removed from her ears, wrists, ankles, neck and who knows where else.

As parents, we make decisions about our children every minute of every day. As children, when our parents become our 'children' we find ourselves in the same role. We ask ourselves the classic questions: If I put Dad/Mom in a nursing home or care facility, will they be angry with me? Will he/she be cared for adequately? How will we afford this? Should I, instead, bring him/her into my own home and provide care here? These questions become more complicated when there are other siblings or members of the family who have various opinions. This often leads to animated discussions and uncomfortable decisions.

I have a cousin who, like me, is the oldest of her other two siblings. She is a very accomplished, professional woman who was assigned the responsibility of caring for her mother, who was living with Alzheimer's syndrome. One of her siblings was unable to care for the mother, and the other was unwilling. My cousin, eventually, placed her mother in a nursing home, where she was able to visit her every day. Of course, as is the case with most Alzheimer's sufferers, the mother no longer recognized the daughter, or anyone else. Nevertheless, my cousin faithfully attended to her mother every day until she eventually died in her 90's.

Decisions as to how to 'parent' your parents are often painful and lead to further irritation among family members. This often leads to fatigue and resentment; sometimes reports emerge of elder care abuse or abuse of the caregiver by the elder or other family members.

There are many resources available in print and on the web regarding elder care abuse and caring for the caregivers. It is important, if you are the one receiving care or the one giving it, that you be aware of the signs and symptoms and different types of abuse. Abuse of elders takes many different forms involving intimidation or threats, neglect or financial crimes. Some elders and their caregivers are more at risk than others. As elders become fragile, they are less able to fend off bullying or fight back when being physically attacked. Mental and physical ailments can contribute to an atmosphere in the home that invites unscrupulous people to take advantage of the elderly. More than half a million reports of abuse against elderly Americans reach authorities every year, and millions more cases go unreported.

Caregivers who become overwhelmed or stressed can be prone to bouts of depression, impatience, feeling abandoned and unsupported, and, eventually, anger. If the caregiver is fortunate enough to have other family members to share the responsibilities or give them some time off from the daily routines, they are unique. So many times distant family members think they are being helpful when, in reality, they are just adding stress to an already overloaded list of tasks. Having to make a meal for the visiting family, who have come to 'help' is not support for the caregiver. Even having to prepare a guest room or shop for the needs of visitors is an added burden. What I found most helpful was to tell the family helpers that I will be gone during their visit. That way, I got a much needed break, and they learned, first-hand, the moment by moment realities that I faced in the ensuing weeks or months between their visits.

Anger, when appropriately placed and expressed, can be helpful and therapeutic. I came very close to expressing my anger/frustration at Bella when she repeatedly broke the toilet in her bathroom. Time after time, I was summoned over to the house, sometimes in the middle of the night, because, once again, Bella had cracked the seal on the floor or the entire bowl or tank. Older people, who cannot sit down or stand up without assistance, often fall onto toilets and cannot get up without railings or help. So, after we had replaced numerous wax seals and toilets, and installed railings, I had had enough! That was the beginning of the bathroom toilet and floor replacement, which became a total remodel of the bathroom, which became a $200,000 redesign of the entire house. This, of course, meant that Bella had to go.

After three years, and hourly, daily care, Bella moved to a care facility in a near-by big city. She was now closer to her other children, her doctors, and her new-found friends, whom she quickly acquired in the building. Today, when she says "We..." she no longer means THE FAMILY. She now refers to her NEW family as the other gals and 'boys' down the hall or in the common room. This only child, who prided herself on being a steadfast widow, now relates how the 'boys' flirt with her and how 'cute' this one or that one is. She involves herself with the sagas of hospitalizations and loneliness of her 'friends'.

I take special note of Bella's present adventures. We will all be there, someday.

BOOMER ANGST

You know those jokes that pass around the internet that start with...."You know you're getting older when..."? There should be a whole series that start with..."You know it's a myth about retirement when..." Or, have I just reinvented the AARP magazine? In any event, approaching 63 and being retired leaves one with a lot of thinking to do. No matter what I busy myself with each day (yesterday's delight was thinning the rows of salad greens in the vegetable garden), I do a lot of remembering. Flipping through the photo gallery in my mind of my memories of diverse families, I see the convent of nuns that taught at our parochial school. I see them in their black and white habits, hands hidden away in modesty, single file, crossing the playground in ankle deep snow, on their way to morning mass. Mother Superior is at the head of the line. Following her, are nine or ten of her 'children'. The parish priest, Father, greets Mother and leads them into the stalls at the front of the congregation. All of a sudden, a long forgotten song pops into my brain as if I was right back there at St. Dominic's Catholic School in the 6th grade, 1959.

Sister Mary Claire was a petite, pretty Nun. She had the most beautiful complexion, and, I surmised, silky blonde hair hiding under that coif or wimple or whatever esoteric name they called those contraptions. She was shy and demure in every way except when it came to belting out a song, or getting us 6th graders to do it. One day she stormed into the classroom with a determined look and began teaching us an unmistakable propagandized military march. She said that it would be the future theme song of our assemblies and that we were going to learn it and sing it for the Pastor of the church soon.

Now, imagine the actor that played the Cowardly Lion in the movie, "The Wizard of OZ". I think his name was Burt Lahr. Can you still hear him singing his trademark solo? "IFIIIII were KIIIING of the FFOREEEST…not duke, not prince, not knight!" He mocked the false vibrato that was so popular in those corny movies of the '30's and '40's. Now, imagine a marching song not unlike the kind that would come out of the mouths of Hitler Youth. And, imagine a voice with exaggerated intonations, like Burt Lahr would give it, singing this brain washing song that we had to learn:

"AN ARMY OF YOUTH FIGHTING FOR STANDARDS OF TRUTH; WE'RE FIGHTING FOR CHRIST THE LORD. HEADS LIFTED HIGH, CATHOLIC ACTION OUR CRY, AND THE CROSS OUR ONLY SWORD. COMRADES TRUE NEATH THE HUE OF THE RED, WHITE AND BLUE. FOR OUR FAITH, FOR OUR FLAG, FOR CHRIST THE KING."

We might as well have been goose-stepping around the classroom led by Sister Mary Claire, whose face was turning bright red with the excitement of it all.

"WE LIFT OUR HANDS; THE KING COMMANDS; WE THROW OUR FORTUNES TO THE LORD. MARY'S

SON TILL THE WORLD IS WON, WE WILL PLEDGE
TO HIS LOYAL WORD."

Of course, all this contra-Nazi music style went right over my
head and I belted the song out along with all those other future nuns and priests, soldiers and brides of Christ. 'DAUN-
TLESSLY ON WE SWING FOR CHRIST THE KING!'
How many 6th graders know what the word 'dauntlessly'
means?

These many years later, when I read tabloids that report
'shocking' stories of youth leaving their families to join crazy
cults, I smile and say to myself, "Get over it"! I am here to
tell you that you can escape a cult and survive to tell the tale.
When I see two milky-complexioned Mormon boys in white
shirts and black ties walking down the street on their mission,
I say to myself, "Ah, life is wasted on the young". When I
read in the local paper of the aspirations of a senior boy who
plans to go to Bible College next year so that he can be a
minister some day, I say to myself, "Gee, I hope some sexy
young thing comes along to change his mind".

The world doesn't need any more goose-stepping religious
youth. And, years after Sister Mary Claire taught us that song,
I ran into her in a bar. She had left the convent. Like so many
of us, she had exchanged her convent family for another.
Leaning into the arms of her lover, her silky blond hair, now
flecked with gray, she could still belt out a tune. This time, I
sang along with her "Inagadadavida, baby. Doncha know that
I really love you"? Somehow, she had lost the Burt Lahr

thing. Neath the hue of the neon fluorescent blue, she swung dauntlessly on, following a different cause.

CLAUDE - THIRD FAMILY

My first long-term relationship after college, in 1971, was with an Aquarian named Claude. He was originally from the South. His Savannah, Georgian accent accompanied a puckish face, framed in blond hair. He loved grits, new cars, designing interiors of homes, and unknown to me for the nearly 3 years we were together, sex with other men on the side. Certainly, guiding spirits were watching over me. When one of my best friends finally told me of Claude's penchant for bus station bathrooms, the light bulb came on and I saw, once again, that we were not going to remain a family.

Before that salient bit of information was shared with me, I was doe-eyed in love with this older man, Claude. He was smooth and sophisticated with a southern accent that could charm your pants off. And, apparently, that is exactly what he did with lots of men and women besides me. Claude was bisexual. When I met him, I learned that he had fathered a child with a woman who still lived in our town. She was a model – tall and overly featured. Claude designed her clothes and dressed her; he did her hair and make-up and booked her modeling engagements. Like a lamb to the slaughter, I marveled at his talents and planned ahead for the next forty or fifty years of our lives together.

Being in the building years of my career as an educator, I applied for a grant from a prestigious Foundation in New York City. I became a finalist and flew to the Big Apple during Christmas break, 1973. When I came home to Claude, he seemed strangely quiet. Cleaning our bedroom several days later, I found a pair of women's panties under our bed. Confronted with this, Claude admitted that he had had this woman, the mother of his child, over for sex while I had been gone. I never regained trust or confidence, and, several months later, learning the news of his other dalliances, I decided it was time to end this relationship and move out. Just like in the monastery break-up, I cried for days, grieving the loss of this family.

Several years later, and many ensuing years of happiness with Joel, we heard the sad news that Claude had died of AIDS. AIDS had taken almost all of my friends. Again, only by some mysterious intervention from my guiding spirits, was I spared of this heart-breaking disease. Joel and I spent many years working privately as well as officially in organizations that gave support to people living with HIV. Out of our grief and fear, we became deeply involved in one particular organization that had risen out of the ashes of devastation created by the AIDS epidemic in San Francisco.

The group was called SHANTI, a Sanskrit word that means 'inner peace'. We were an eclectic assortment of educators, medical professionals, guidance counselors and good-hearted souls, both gay and straight, who wanted to do something rather than standing by watching everyone die. We met in small groups, once a week, with a trained leader, to share our experiences. After a deeply life-changing training session, we were each assigned a client who was living, and subsequently, in those days, dying of AIDS. We would remain with this person until they finally passed. The small group meetings once a week were for mutual support as we, in turn, supported our clients through their processes. It became a consuming dedication. Joel eventually rose to be the volunteer coordinator. We spent hours each week taking our clients to doctor appointments, shopping, hospitals, and walks in the park. We cooked meals for our clients and arranged for MEALS ON WHEELS to deliver food to those who were in need.

One by one, each volunteer would report, at the group support meeting, that another client had died.

When we were ready, we would be assigned one more person to care for until they passed. Most of my clients were humble, grateful individuals. Many of them had been abandoned by their families. An older man who had been an educator, married, with children, was shunned by his brother and parents. His ex-wife stood by him till the end. When he died, his brother placed all his belongings in storage so that they could 'cool down' and disinfect from the AIDS virus. Another one of my clients insisted on spending all his money on one last world cruise. Too ill to really enjoy the traveling, he returned home with his partner and immediately died.

A common trait shared by all the people that we supported in our SHANTI years was that they were not angry. They did not blame anyone or hold a grudge. Some of them frittered away their last days partying in denial. Some became spiritual and looked internally. Many of them were dazed and in shock. None of them came across as saints or martyrs. They were common, everyday people with families, careers, and lives coming to a screeching halt, often with very little warning.

When my best friend of more than 20 years, Maurice, died of AIDS, I had had enough. I just could not take it anymore. I started blocking out all information on the TV, radio, magazines and newspapers on anything having to do with the topic of AIDS. It crushed me; it sucked the air out of my soul. I had no more energy to face one more person in my life dying. It would be many years before I could gather the courage to learn how the epidemic had progressed, and who else I knew had been taken. I had gone underground, and when I surfaced, the landscape was post-nuclear. Most of what had been familiar to me was vaporized.

Re-inventing ME meant honoring the anniversaries of the lives and events that had shaped who I had become. I had not arrived at this place alone. I now had a family with Joel and our boys who gave deep, honest meaning to my life. That changed everything. My partner and I began to notice that people who were not participating in family life started leaving us out. We received fewer invitations to dinner and parties. Our circle of friends included other couples like us who had adopted or who were creating intentional extended family situations. Our own bio-families struggled to define what we were doing. They were confused and hurt by our strong, close and successful family. We had rounded a corner and there was no turning back.

There is not one, single definition of FAMILY. At this point, I know what family is not, and I know what family is for me and my partner. I know how families in my past have hurt and healed me. There is no perfect family. Perhaps there is no imperfect family. Your closest, dearest committed family, my family, is what it is today. Only we can decide if we want to remain in the moment with a particular family. As my friend, Ann, says, "We only have this moment."

One of my personal heroes, Christopher Isherwood, talks about how everything is as it is meant to be. Life is the task of growing the courage and clarity to see our path. In this incarnation, we have the opportunity to be open to our teachers and the lessons toward enlightenment. We can embrace our families with light and unconditional love and forgiveness. It is not too late to create the family configuration we want, the family that is just right for us, today.

MAURICE

Maurice was the last of a kind. Unless he opened his mouth, at least in the early days, he looked like a cross between a mountain man, Louis XIV, a sumo wrestler and your pastor. But, when he spoke, there was no question in your mind that this guy was like no one you had ever met or ever imagined. He stood about 5'8", jet black hair, a rock-hard prominent jaw covered with a thick black beard. He was solid muscle with stocky legs right off a grand piano. His voice could be shrill, effeminate, booming or paralyzing. He had the most annoying cackling laugh that could, and often did, fill a movie theatre. His laugh either made others laugh or want to strangle him. He was a self-proclaimed asocial, self-ish, sex addict with no conscience. I thought he was the most social and socially appropriate person I had ever met. He threw dinner parties every night of the week for the local rich and famous, yet never had a dime to his name. People found him either repulsive or irresistible. There was no middle ground with Maurice; you either loved him or hated him. His collection of capes, canes, walking sticks and kimonos was legendary. I never knew anyone who had more hats, top hats, berets, or scarves than Maurice. Maurice invented the term 'panache'.

I was introduced to Maurice at a Christmas party in 1969. He was costumed in an outfit that made him resemble an actor in an old vampire movie. He moved around the food table in spats, black cape, vest with pocket watch – one of his signature accessories – black bowtie, authentically tied by his nibs

– and a top hat perched on his shoulder-length black hair that framed his milky-white skin and alarmingly handsome face. Maurice appeared to have no pores in his skin. His full red lips and hypnotic smile masked really bad teeth, and often accompanying bad breath. The vampire analogy seems to fit him best. He would have been proud of it.

Although Maurice and I had a brief, playful affair, we were destined to be best friends, not lovers. It was he who introduced me to my first partner, Claude. Ironically, they would both die of AIDS within a year of each other in the early 90s.

Maurice was born December 2nd, 1948. His parents were farmers who literally came across the prairies to Washington State in covered wagons. Maurice was their one and only child, who they spawned late in life. Most of his friends thought his parents were his grandparents. Until they moved into town of after Maurice's birth, they had probably never used indoor plumbing or electricity. To say they were poor was a compliment to their survival instincts and talents as true pioneers. After finding a piece of land out in the Valley, Terrance, Maurice's father, built their humble house by himself and set up family life as best he knew how to do without the surrounds of a farm. Lena, or Sarah, as she was sometimes called, preferred to cook on a wood stove, canned, raised chickens and kept a vegetable garden. Terrance raised goats and hunted in the woods for whatever meat they would eat. Maurice was given a pet skunk by his doting parents, taught to fish, hunt, sew, sing and cook. At his local elementary school, the cooks, recognizing the dire conditions of his displaced family, gave him free lunch. He used to tell me how exciting it was to get chocolate milk and Jell-O on his tray at school – exotic delicacies that they could never afford at his home.

The first time that Maurice invited me to meet his parents and have dinner at their house I was given a tour of the place. Concrete floors, with some area rugs, went throughout the 4 rooms: Terrance and Sarah's bedroom, a living/dining area, a kitchen and Maurice's bedroom with the one bathroom. The walls were concrete block, even the shower, no tub, was concrete block. No paint on the walls, no TV – just a radio – and kerosene lamps. This was 1970. Maurice and I were nearly 22; yet being at his parents' home was like stepping back into a history that I barely recognized from books and old photos. This was a family like those I had only read about or had seen in vintage movies. His parents were the real McCoy, no other agenda, what you saw was what you got!

This was a family of unconditional love. Maurice was so proud of his parents and his heritage that you would have thought he descended from royal lineage. That evening, at the table, Sarah placed a huge platter with an aluminum dome in the center. "Terrance, will you carve the roast"? This must be some massive roast under that covering. I was prepared to be impressed. From what I perceived, I did not expect the Ashleys to be able to provide a roast of that proportion to one of Maurice's newest friends. They were not pretentious people at all.

Terrance stepped forward with carving knife in hand. He ceremoniously lifted the cover to reveal the roast: a hamburger meatloaf the size of my fist. It was a special meal, and I had been invited to share it with them.

Maurice was a HOBBIT freak. His apartments were re-enactments of the Shire, the Sylvan forest, and everything Gandalf. Later in his life, he would move toward New-Age crystals, Buddhist kitsch, and everything India. He also fancied himself Mormon, Jewish, Episcopalian, and Quaker. Maurice was happy at whatever religious rite he was attending as long as he could wear the appropriate cultural costume, complete with incense, bells, ram's horns for calling the dead, and marigold-flower garlands. It wasn't uncommon to see him in blue eye-shadow and lipstick, while chopping wood or helping a friend build an outhouse.

One summer we traveled together to Guadalajara, Mexico, where he had been a teacher in an International School. He had waist length hair at the time, which he decided to shave off at the half-way mark from the middle of his head to the front, looking somewhat like a Japanese Samurai warrior. Every time he took his hat off in the wilting Mexican heat, busloads of school children would burst out laughing, which hurt his feelings. At the Catholic cathedral famous for its healing Virgin in Patzcuaro, Maurice climbed the long staircase to her shrine on his knees, begging her to heal him from being HIV positive.

At the end of our stay in the Michoacán, we joined Joel and other friends in Puerto Vallarta, where Maurice had also lived for a time. We rented a villa, complete with a maid, Maria, who kept re-arranging all our personal affects. Maurice, who was fairly fluent in Spanish, told her to leave our stuff alone. She ignored him and continued to insist on hiding shaving gear, socks, and anything else she thought was out of place. When she washed our bed sheets, she dried them on the tile roof of her house. Maurice held court there, as usual, spending all our money, since he had none of his own. A few years later, he made one more trip back to Mexico with a new boyfriend. He was quite ill at the time. Apparently, the Virgin of Patzcuaro had not blessed him.

In 1990, Maurice's health was going down fast. He had lived off and on with Joel and me over the years. Sometimes he had his own place, but mostly he shared digs and expenses with more affluent associates who could keep him in the lifestyle to which he had trained them to be accustomed. At the end, after moving heaven and earth to set up a 'salon' in his home where he wanted to die, he suddenly decided to return to the hospital. On the evening of November 15th, 1990, Joel and my 16th anniversary, he died in the company of three of his long-time friends. I had visited him the day before. He had opened his eyes as I approached his bed, and he mouthed the words, "I love you", and then closed his eyes for the last time.

Being the executor of his will and having durable power of attorney over his estate was a messy process. He had no estate. However, all his friends, to whom he had promised the moon and the stars upon his death, were sure he did have one, and were going to squeeze the blood out of the stone, if it killed me. It took me a while to convince them otherwise, and, in the meantime, my staying power on the project faded. I did manage to have an ash-scattering ceremony for him and our friends out at Greyrose on a warm spring day. He had requested that a good bit of his ashes be placed inside a brass Buddha, which I still have. His idea was that this statue containing his ashes would travel from house to house of those who had loved him. I never really got around to sending the statue on tour, and no one ever asked about it.

Maurice's mother and father had long since passed on. I remember being almost killed in a close encounter with a semi-truck on Stevens Pass returning on an icy, snowy night from his mother's funeral in their home town. His father lived a few more years. I drove Maurice over to see him for the last time. We loaded a desk into my car, which we still use in our house, and Maurice shed quiet tears almost all the way back home.

Even though, technically, I was older than Maurice by a month, he was a like a big brother or father figure to me. He was wise, never ashamed and a fierce protector of those he considered to be part of his family. We had a pact that if there was ever any way, after he died, he would give me a sign that he was in contact. I asked him what that sign would be, and he said that it would be the number '5'.

A month after Maurice died, Joel and I bought a Co-Op apartment on Capitol Hill. Its address was A-5. 19 days after Maurice left this planet in November, our second son, was born on Dec. 3rd. Although he never met Maurice, there is an uncanny resemblance and many of Maurice's extreme mannerisms are present in our son's personality. One day, I laid out several pieces of jewelry on a bed, some of which had been Maurice's. I told our son to choose one thing that he wanted to keep. He immediately chose a watch-fob that Maurice had attached to one of his many pocket watches. Nothing else interested him; he didn't even know what a pocket watch was.

Yep, we made a family, all right.

A NIGHT IN A BAD INN

"Life is a night in a bad inn" – St. Theresa of Avila

Every so often Mistress Fate seduces me back to my roots. Like an old addiction, I find myself compelled, either by co-incidence or duty, to return to the town where I mostly grew up. When I was growing up there, even then, I read about a somewhat famous local author who referred to our little city as "…that colorless town". After graduating from high school and fleeing to a monastery in California for three years, the home town habit sucked me back to finish my un-dergraduate college degree. Drawn by my grandparents' gen-erous offer of money to pay my tuition, I enrolled at the local private University for another lethal dose of Catholicism and bourgeois indoctrination. This was a repeat of the initial in-oculation of my Prep school years. Upon graduation from college, I was sentenced to an additional stay of 3 years. In that time, I taught junior high school students how to read and write and, most importantly, to think. I still carry in my wallet a laminated note from a student of that era who gushed, "Dear Mr. Martin. I write now to tell you how much I appreciated some of the things you taught me. I love, I thrive on imagery and symbolism in everything. I fear that I, as well as many others, had no appreciation whatsoever for those things as well as education as a whole. Thanks, Mr. Martin, it's become a great part of my life, sincerely, 'River' ".

And so it is that I found myself, at the age of sixty, returning to serve another, albeit brief, sentence in this Bad Inn at the State School Directors Association Annual Conference. An overnight in that colorless town would be tolerable, but three nights there requires deep catharsis and more wine than I would be able to politely consume in the presence of my colleagues.

Mingling at the conference, I felt like a salmon swimming upstream. Everyone else was decked out in administration uniform: tasseled shoes, Nordstrom slacks, ties, jackets, and shirts so starched at the dry cleaners that I winced for their discomfort whenever they moved. I, on the other hand, intentionally selected outfits that were beyond casual: hemp pants, bison-leather clogs, yellow tennis shoes, and lots of corduroy. That, and the diamond studs in both ears announced to the other salmon in the stream: HEY! What the hell! Life is too short! Look forward to another life, NOW!

I do understand, however, why most of those people are doing what they are doing. After all, I was in that club just a few years ago. I do not judge them: I do not advise them. I hope for them that they will emerge on the other side minimally scarred and less damaged than I am.

Finally Saturday morning arrived. I wanted to meet my nemesis. I wanted to face my memories of the past. I walked the streets of Downtown on a bright blue-sky Saturday morning. I stepped out in my Territory Ahead outfit, diamond earstuds, cell phone, credit cards, and my new digital camera.

One block off the main street I was in a foreign land: more street people and homeless than I had ever seen in other cities of similar size, more wheelchairs, more amputees and people sleeping under blue tarps than I ever expected. The morning headlines in the local newspaper warned that the City Council was going to crack down on transients and beggars. I wondered how and why?

Soon, I walked past the building where I attended my first drag ball. At the time, I was working for Sears, and my boss invited me to his coming out party there as a drag queen. I remember being so dazzled by the event and his audacity. Now, the building is in ruins, about to be razed. Walking on, I passed familiar sites, building after building in foreclosure and for sale. For sale: The Colonial Hotel, premier landmark in days gone by. In foreclosure: Peters' Clothing Store. I remember the priest who counseled my mother about my entrance to my all boy's Prep school. He told her that, above all, I needed to have the best clothing in order to be accepted at my high school – thus a trip to Peters' clothing store. Later, I learned that one of my favorite Aunts had an affair with Mr. Peters, that ended in scandal. Small world.

Next, I found myself standing in front of the FEDERAL COURTHOUSE on Main Street. The irony is that this place is where I was first rejected by my government. In 1971, at the height of the Viet Nam War, I drew a very high lottery number for the Draft. Dutifully, I showed up for the indignity of the Army physical: spread your cheeks for the ultimate humiliation. In the end, no pun intended, I was summoned to the chief officer's quarters and, flanked by his body guards and several American flags, as if I threatened him, he informed me that I was unsuitable for service, since I had 'checked the box' admitting that I was a homosexual. He told me never to contact them again and that I would be contacted by them. Amen. Good bye. Get out. Did they know that many of the most well-known members of high society families in the '50's and '60's were alleged to be some of the most notorious queens to those who knew Dorothy? Many men told of trysts with these fellows, a few of whom were follow graduates of my Prep school. It is amazing how big the closet can become when the truth be known.

Down the block I found a street couple who were sitting on a bench in front of a public park. They were covered in boils and scabs. They were in their twenties. She smiled at me, revealing teeth that had not been brushed in months. He had his pant legs rolled up to his knees, revealing sores and wounds that needed serious medical attention. It was thirty-five degrees, yet they were cheery and lucent. I asked them if I could take their picture. "For 50 cents," he offered. "OK" I snapped a couple shots. "Hey, mister, for $2.50 you can take another picture." "How about if I give you a couple cigarettes and five bucks"? "Yeah, you've made our day! Do you want me to show you my Mohawk? Here"! He threw his cap on the ground and he and she posed. I mentioned that it was cold, and she said, "No matter; we are going to hell anyway so it will be warm there". I hoped it would not be soon, not tonight, not ever. Her unwashed teeth looked like they had been treated with braces at some time in her youth. He spoke with an educated drawl. Her eyes had a spark of knowledge and choice. They were on some journey that I could only peek at from the shutter of my camera. A little farther down the street I read a poster, picturing a transient man in distress; the caption read – DON'T LOOK DOWN ON ANYONE UNLESS YOU ARE WILLING TO LEND THEM A HAND UP.

A little further down, I noticed the title on a building: SAR-DUCCI AND ASSOCIATES. I had attended high school with Dave Sarducci. He was another Italian boy whose family was out of my family's league. I wished him and his associates well. I passed another building that announced: WHEAT-LAND BANK – YOUR MONEY IS SAFE WITH US. Yeah, right. Had they not read the headlines this morning and the stock market reports?

The one thing that I was not able to do in my inducted pilgrimage back to my hometown was to visit my grandparents' graves: Uomo and Alma, Italian immigrants to the New World. He was born in 1895, came to America in 1912. She was chosen by him in his return visit to Italy in 1925, and Bella, their only child, was born back in the States in 1927. My parents celebrated their marriage in the Colonial Hotel, even then a fashionable place for such events. Today, it remains, after much restoration, the focal luxury reminder of the town's distant past.

As I returned to my hotel for checkout, I passed a run-down building that displayed a billowing banner telling anyone interested that this luxury condominium was for sale – inquire within. I looked out at the vast empty parking lot and streets that invited a cannon blast with no repercussions, and I wondered who would respond to that ad.

Things change. Life changes everything and everyone. Nothing remains the same anywhere else. This town, with all its families of every description struggling to survive, somehow remains the same. I still see Davey and Billy and Tim walking with me down the middle of the street on a winter's evening. We have just come out of a Boy Scout meeting full of our selves. We walk down the street, peeing on the yellow line. It is just a laugh.

As I returned to my hotel, I wished Davey, Billy and Tim good luck. I hoped that they were not still living there, unless they were very wealthy. I looked forward to my flight back home at the edge of the world, the edge of forgiveness and color. There is lots of color where I live. Every night the sun splashes color on my dogs and Joel and me as we walk on the beach.

ANNIVERSARIES MAKE ME CRY

I read somewhere that taking naps extends your life. I am trying but, It didn't work for me today. Haunted by the upcoming anniversary of my first retirement, I had to get up and write this.

Next month will mark the anniversary of my first retirement. I have been having nightmares and daymares about the cast of characters that flowed through my career years and precipitated my early retirement. I probably could have lasted a couple more years if it wasn't for the vicious, mean-spirited nut-cakes that plagued my existence as a school principal. As a result of my chosen profession, I have ruined my health, and stored visions of these vindictive weirdoes in my brain forever.

I know there are people for whom working is like breathing. They get up every morning, go off somewhere for 8 or 9 hours and come home like it is no big deal. Work for them is a silly accident that happened to interrupt a perfectly wonderful childhood, so they do their best to ignore the entire process. These are the same people who live into their 90's laughing at corny jokes and marveling at the newfangled inventions that their grandchildren are playing with. I'm not one of these people.

I attacked the unexamined life with a vengeance. My father died at 58, burning himself out on cigarettes and alcohol. I will probably suffer a similar fate, burning myself out asking questions, reliving conversations and arguments, and wishing I had made smarter decisions. Actually, the truth is that I wish I were a little more stupid and brain-dead than I am. The bliss of ignorance could be gratefully anaesthetizing.

Predominately, aside from pesky teacher characters I met over the years like Jim Swanson, who probably still has not figured out his sexual orientation, Geraldine Carey, who couldn't decide to grieve me or love me, the Smith parents who were twin voices to the Superintendent about everything I said, didn't say, farted or otherwise, and a few nasty, born-from-the-movie "The Exorcist" students, my skin crawls from knowing two individuals in particular.

The first of these nightmares was a tragically unhappy woman named Buffy Dover. She had probably been a cheerleader both in high school and college. Since then, she had put on a little weight – let's say 100+ lbs., mostly in her boobs. She liked to wriggle them, wiggle them, rub them and swing them in my direction.

When it finally dawned on her that I wasn't going for the bait, she decided that I must be destroyed. She was trapped in an unhappy marriage with a very rich car-dealer husband. Long since had the embers of their love died. She was now married to her job, come hell or high water, or me! It took her 4 years, but she developed a Strategic Plan to get rid of me. It killed her when I beat her to the punch and found a job elsewhere. All she could do was write me a poisoned letter in the end and deliver it when she was sure I could not respond officially.

I especially remember a vacation day over Christmas break. I thought I was the only working fool in the building, but when Buffy entered my office, I knew I should have known better. She leaned toward me over my desk, her enormous bosoms hanging in my paperwork, and began to tell me her opinion about everything and everyone. Since, in her mind, this one-way conversation was 'off the record', she let it all fly. She was the kind of person who could be dirty to the core one minute, and the Virgin Mary the next. In fact, she was a Catholic – the worst kind of hypocrite – church on Sunday, First Communion and Confirmation classes for her kids, and then plotting character assassination of her boss later that afternoon over the phone with other like-minded vampire teachers.

The second person, who, just by coincidence happened to be a woman and a Catholic AND a woman with a fetish about her breasts, was also a teacher with a mission to hate everyone who intended to be her 'boss'. Estelle Jones was the pillar of her neighborhood community: a churchgoer, a brownie and cookie baker, a mom, a Girl Scout leader, and a stealth bomber who moved underground against all who got in her way, and who didn't like her rubbing her breasts on them. She, like Buffy, was a Republican. I admit I do not understand how anyone who is a woman, a black person, a gay person, a poor person or a teacher can be a Republican. I mean, is that the oxymoron of the universe? Someone please explain to me how a teacher could have loyal affection for politicians who would love nothing more than to see them vaporized. I don't get it.

Estelle couldn't spell, read, follow a logical conversation or understand most two-syllable vocabulary words. How she attained a teaching certificate boggles my mind and only adds gasoline to the already burning inferno of my day and night-mares. She was loud and always guffawing about things that were funny only to her. She was the most righteous person I have ever met: completely convinced that she was right in her pinhead opinions and everyone else who disagreed with her was evil and a pervert – especially me. Most notably, she dolloped her opinions generously on her lessons and her students. Whatever had caught her attention on TV the previous evening was the subject of her lesson plan for the next day: 911/Sex-Predators/Stem Cell Research/Oil/Gay Marriage/Abortion/Etc. When God had said she could be a social studies teacher, he/she gave her permission to talk about anything she wanted. That was her belief, and when I got in the way of that, another Strategic Plan was born to ruin my career.

There were other individuals, including my own bosses – some of them inept, unqualified ladder-climbers for whom I blushed every time they opened their mouths. There were the so-called consultants, charging arms and legs to tell me and my staff the obvious. There were zombies and sycophants and actors and ghouls and they all rush across the stage of my dreams. There I am, in a tug-of-war for my soul – me on one end and they on the other pushing and pulling for the prize: my memories and fears.

The stage goes black; the actors are now naked, as am I, and we are all equal. We are all silent and rehearsing our lines. How will we explain what happened? How will we justify intentional genocide of our life's work? When will the curtain finally fall on this misguided stupidity? We were so smug thinking we knew the ultimate truth of research and experience. We laid it on those innocent children, suffocating them with our knowledge. Years later, I still stager to the breakfast table in the morning, so relieved that the demon dreams of the night are behind me.

WE'RE A FAMILY, ALRIGHT

In 1991, Tom Spanbauer published his best seller, *The Man Who Fell in Love with the Moon*. Joel and I have had a long standing tradition of reading books, aloud, to each other. We often do this while traveling in the car, or when we go to bed. *Watership Down*, *The Plague Dogs*, *Fly Away Paul*, various ecological and scientific books, books with gay themes and biographies have been among our list of read-aloud sharing. The moment we started reading *The Man Who Fell in Love with the Moon*, we both were smitten with the characters in the story, and the familiar setting. And, we both fell in love with the author. I felt I knew Tom Spanbauer. I imagined talking with him, laughing and even sleeping with him. In addition, with the story set in Northern Idaho and Montana, places where we loved to explore and play, we began imagining that we recognized particular locations, bars, streets and buildings.

There probably isn't a less likely town to attract two gay guys than Wallace, Idaho. Famous for 19th century mining disasters and accompanying whore houses, the town is nestled in a narrowing canyon on I-90. At one time, in the late 1800's, it boasted the first electric street lamps, paved sidewalks, a sewer system and a damn fine Victorian train station, that has since been moved a few blocks away to accommodate the freeway. Main street looks like a movie set for "The Gun Slinger" or "High Noon". Tall facades on wooden store fronts, ornate gingerbread gee-gaws and stairways climbing up the sides of the canyon to homes perched in the woods on the hills are the scenery you drink in. It is one of those relics of old towns that make you drunk with not knowing where to look next; you are surrounded with photo ops.

West of town, as the valley widens out a bit, sits the residential district, developed by rich miners and loggers who came here to settle, raise their families, and find their fortunes. Each house is unique and, even though real families still live real lives in many of them, there are a few that are opened up to the public for tours. Walking through these homes on a hot Idaho summer afternoon, you can almost hear the dishes being scraped in the pantry, and you can smell the homey reminders of pie and coffee followed by cigars and brandy out on the broad, veranda porches.

Late in that summer of 1991, as we neared the end of Spanbauer's book, we were certain that we knew exactly where the scenes of the book were set. Our first son was out on his own, and we had not yet adopted our second. So, in-between children, and having some vacation time on our hands, we loaded up the car with book in hand and headed for Wallace, Idaho, and points beyond.

We stayed at the Starlight Motel, on the edge of the downtown district. We ate at Fong's diner and had a beer in the old saloon. We visited the historic graveyard on the outskirts of town, combing for clues of deceased persons from the book. An influenza epidemic had wiped out half the town's population at the turn of the century. This was followed by a tragic fire that burned down most of the original pioneer buildings.

We followed the creek bed, the scene of so many antics in the book. And, after thoroughly convincing ourselves that we had uncovered those mysteries, we headed for the place of one of the most dramatic scenes in the plot: Flathead Lake in Montana.

If you have ever been to Flathead Lake, it is not hard to imagine what it must have been like when Native American tribes camped on its banks and fished in its waters. Osprey still nest along the shore in tall trees. The waters are warm in last August, attracting other birds of prey and harboring large, lazy trout. Unfortunately now, suburban civilization has encroached on the gently sloping hillsides that reach down to the shores. Houses, wineries, gas stations and Indian gambling joints are everywhere. We managed to find a quiet campground and a site right next to a good swimming hole.

After setting up our tent and taking a much needed swim, we knew why we had been drawn to this very spot. It was getting dark. Swigging shots of whiskey, we crawled into our tent with a flashlight and long into the night read aloud the final chapters of the book – laughing, crying, holding each other and finishing off the bottle. Shed and Delwood had slept there. Ida had sunned herself on the beach there. The spirit of the man who fell in love with the moon danced around our tent all night and followed us the next day as we deadheaded our way back to Seattle and our jobs.

About two or three months later, we read that Tom Spanbauer was going to do a book talk and sign copies in a local bookstore in Seattle. We showed up early, soaked in every word that came out of his rugged, handsome face and that big, big wounded heart. When it was our turn in line, we handed him our book and told him our story of Wallace and Flathead Lake, finishing the final chapters by flashlight, tipsy in our tent. He rose up out of his chair and took our hands in his, looking each of us directly in the eyes. Time seemed to stop; I went temporarily deaf as I could hear nothing else in the store but his words, "Thank You".

Above his autograph at the front of our book, the author wrote, "Yep, we're family all right"!

FAMILY HOLIDAYS

OK I'll admit it. I am absolutely addicted to holiday TV ads. The minute Halloween is over, I am scanning the networks for the first advertisements with schmaltzy background music, snowflakes, and animated elves. The more sentimental they are, the better. By Thanksgiving I have placed a permanent box of tissue on the arm of my chair for those 'family' ads – you know, the ones where everyone is watching out the steamy windows of an architectural digest home, waiting for that last person to slog through the snow, up the path, through the front door, into the waiting arms of grandma and grandpa and all the nieces and nephews. Cut to the Christmas table, laden with the biggest, most perfect turkey you have seen since last year's ads. My eyes start to puddle up as soon as the soldier boy pulls a gift for his mom out of his duffle bag. In the background you hear Harry Connick, Jr. crooning "I'll Be Home For Christmas". I'm on my third tissue as the little girl looks up into her dad's eyes and says, "Can we buy something for Uncle Ted at Wal Mart?" This year I have placed a reserve box of tissue on the floor by the chair for all those "Polar Express" ads. When Joel and our second son and I went to see that movie last Christmas, I cried from the minute the lights went down till we got home in the car hours later. Do they really think I'm going to make it through 60 seconds of the ad for the DVD that comes out next Tuesday with that sweet little poor boy in galoshes and nightshirt running alongside the train? What hope is there for my bleary, swollen eyes when Santa leaves that golden bell on the seat of the sleigh?

Why do they do this to me? Why am I such a sucker for schmaltz? Or am I just feeling sorry for myself because winter is so dark outside all the time? How can a grown man breakdown over ads for Martha Stewart self-lighting trees at Sears or two-for-one wreath sales at Penney's? Maybe it just brings back all the memories of the wonder of color TV back in the early '60s when those ads first started and I watched them during the holidays with my bio-family. My grandfather was the first in our part of town to buy a color TV. Every Sunday evening the whole family would gather at the grandparent's house to watch "The Wonderful World of Disney" in living color.

Addictions to family memories are hard to explain. Any other time of year, I hate the sound of Christmas carols, but right now, I walk around the house humming theme music from "Holiday Happiness" at Target and Mervyn's. Please, I need some relief soon. It's only getting worse, or better, I can't tell which.

Actually, I'm still waiting for that one, best, perfect commercial. It will have to have all the classic elements: snowflakes, tender music, twinkly lights, diamonds in little boxes, families with perfect teeth and immaculately clean and decorated houses, at least one Irish Setter and, oh, how could I forget – the biggest star on top of the most eye-popping Christmas tree ever!

It's a good thing I am retired. I can't tear myself away from the TV these days. What if I missed it? What if I missed the big one I've been waiting for? I don't even know how to set my VCR recorder for this afternoon when I am running out to see if they have the "Polar Express" DVD in the stores yet. Thank goodness they replay these ads over, and over, again and again.

My first memory of a family Christmas celebration is clear and bright, like the star on top of that tree. My uncle, Fabio, a handsome bachelor in his thirties, insisted on tickling me till I cried and nearly threw up. Later that evening, he helped put together a miniature model roller coaster made of tin. There were piles of Italian honey cookies, ribbon candy, spiked eggnog, and, my favorite, cheesecake. That night, after I had been put to bed and the adults were enjoying their drinks and smokes, I snuck down the stairs and raided the dessert table for more cheesecake. To this day, I still can't get enough of that stuff. Food was always a big part of any celebration in the first family. Some of the dishes were special, only to be served on that particular occasion. Unlike contemporary eating habits of present day families, we looked forward to certain treats at Christmas that were not enjoyed at any other feast: turkey, ravioli, gnocchi, tripe, tongue, fruit cake and, of course, cheesecake. Back in the 40's and 50's, most delicacies were seasonal. You could not buy strawberries or watermelon anytime you wanted like you can today. In my present family, we eat any of those things anytime we want.

One Christmas, Joel and I visited friends in Paris for two weeks. When we shopped for the holiday dinner, it felt like the old times. Foie Gras was fresh and made especially for Bonne Noel. Certain wines and liqueurs were marketed only for that time of the year. In England, we had the same experience with Christmas foods. Mince pies, regional apples held back from the shops till a certain day, and fat chickens became once a year prizes for the holiday table.

When I was growing up, my first family opened gifts on Christmas Eve. These days we open our gifts on Christmas morning. Our boys come home for a couple over-nights, gorging on all the bad-for-you treats I put out for them. I like to research unusual recipes, setting the table with the best dishes. The boys don't care about all that – neither does Joel much – so I do it for myself. With that box of tissue close at hand, I busy myself in the kitchen, one eye on the TV ads, one eye watching to see if the cheesecake is ready to be taken out of the oven. I have to be careful not to totally stop what I am cooking to blubber too long, watching jewelry boxes opened under a street lamp with snowflakes fluttering in the background. If I'm not careful, the gravy burns and the cheesecake falls while I hum along "…Every kiss begins with K."

TURNING, TURNING

Life seemed so simple thirty-five years ago. We made decisions unfettered by practical considerations like money,
health, and career. We threw our hearts over the cliff and
leaped over after them. The sunny, cold-crisp day in October
that we drove north of Seattle to look at Greyrose for the
first time was one of those leaps.

It was a simple, one-liner ad in the paper: "Ten acres for sale
in Skykomish valley. If interested call…" We had been looking at various pieces of land all over several counties within
driving distance of the city. Some were hard sells by real estate agents, and others were drive-bys, not worth getting out
of the car. We knew more what we did not want than what
we really wanted. But, we also knew that when we saw the
land that was meant for us, we would know. Our hearts
would open up, and we would be in love.

I recall saying to Joel as I steered the car down the country
road leading to the turn off, "I think we are going to buy this
one." We passed acres of fence posts, loosely related to their
purpose by rusty barbed wire. Cattle and horses glanced our
way unimpressed. Ripe apples clung to scabby trees, already
touched by autumn colors. Others had dropped their loads
onto the road and the car made apple sauce as we winded our
way. We had our first schnauzer, Greta, with us. She was as
anxious to explore as we were. Parking the car at the agreed
upon location, we were dismayed that the seller was not
there, but her jaunty little schnauzer came bounding up to us

and made friends with our Greta. Next, the seller, and soon to be our neighbor and friend, came round the corner with another interested party. Taking one look at us, and at our schnauzer, the seller, a single woman, dismissed the other party with a promise to get back to them, and turned her attention to us. After a long walk around, including a romp to the river that in future years was our friend and angry, flooding enemy, we cinched the deal on the spot.

Thus began a 20 year chapter in our lives that would change the course of our relationship and enrich us and everyone who ever visited Greyrose beyond easy description.

Joel and I have often said that we are living our lives backwards. Most people buy a settle-down home in the city, raise their family, and then look to vacation property or a second home away. We, on the other hand, rented a place in town, bought our property, built our vacation home, and then raised our children. After all of that was secure, we then decided on long-term careers, building the foundation that should have been laid first. Living in this fashion meant translating ourselves to the outside world, and being ready at a moment's notice, to flee to the edge of society where we peered back at what we had bypassed. This meant clinging to each other in ways that other 'normal' couples would not need to do. We were truly 'strangers in a strange land'. Our family was like no other that we knew at that time.

The comforts and also the stress of being so entwined with each other were not without benefits as well as pain. The highs were what made the magic memories; the lows hobbled our abilities to ever be lighthearted and care-free as we see others seemingly are now. When you realize that a fair percentage of society does not approve, not to mention understand your lifestyle, you retreat to the edge on a regular basis to heal and re-strategize.

We learned to speak various other languages, some almost forgotten from our youth. One dialect was used when interacting with other straight families at school and organizations that our sons attended. Another dialect was reserved for clueless neighbors, fellow-workers, service people and contractors who came to our home or phoned to speak to the 'man' of the house or the '…the lady of the house'. Being multi-lingual has its advantages, but it is also exhausting. When you come home, relief takes over and you can finally relax after a day of being a double agent. The payoff is buying legitimacy and credibility; the downside is never feeling whole or honest.

After ten years of life at Greyrose, my father died, and I ran away to escape my first family's expectation that I would become the new Dad. I left with our first son, to teach on a Fulbright, in England. While the experience of living abroad was exhilarating for me and our son, it was unbelievably difficult on Joel, who stayed behind in the States, sacrificing almost everything to support my adventure. Joel visited us four times during that year. Each time, it became increasingly painful to part and be patient for the assignment to come to an end. At the end of a Fulbright assignment, all participants are invited to Tea with a member of the Royal Family. That year, we joined the Queen Mum at Lancaster House, one of the Royal mansions in London. All of us guests were briefed on how to bow or courtesy to the Queen as she passed by us to either shake our hands or make some comment. As I waited my turn, I found myself on one of the many landings as we wound our way up the stairs. On each landing was an enormous pot of what I thought were gallons and gallons of sweet peas. They looked like sweet peas and they smelled like sweet peas, but how could that many sweet peas be assembled in one place? I sidled over to one of the huge urns and pinched a bloom. Yes! They were real! I'll be damned!

Finally, the Queen came to stand in front of me. She was so short and so magnificent. All in powder blue from head to toe, face veiled, she reached out her gloved hand and I touched history. My eyes were cameras: she wore several strands of pearls that were the size of large marbles; on her gloved hand she wore a diamond ring the size of a golf ball; her eyes twinkled and distracted you from the fact that she had really bad teeth, as many British people do. The old gal is dead now, but I understand that she loved her gin and some of her fondest daily companions were the men, other queens, who fixed her drinks and kept her company. I'm not surprised. We all find family in the most interesting ways.

When my son and I returned to the States, I went through a rough adjustment period getting re-accustomed to living with Joel. I had been parenting our first son by myself for a year; he turned 13, entered puberty, ran away at one point, and had his first sexual experience with a girl up in his bedroom while

I was making dinner one evening. Yikes! Joel had gained a lot of weight; his career was taking off while, at the same time, he had to hold Greyrose and all our financial interests together (an exercise which he was not fond of, because that was usually my job), and he was tired of being celibate, waiting for my return. I needed a re-entry period; he needed: "Let's go!"

Another complication in our relationship at the time emerged in the form of 'Gay Pride'. Joel had become a Gay Activist. He was on so many committees and involved in so many causes, that he was gone to a meeting almost every night of the week. So, if we wanted to re-establish familiarity and a family atmosphere, it was challenging to carve out the time to do so. One weekend, my friend Judy and I went to an educator's workshop in another city. It meant that I had to forego attending the Gay Pride Parade that Joel had been deeply involved creating. I resented his involvement and he resented my lack of interest. Judy asked if I felt badly that I was not there to support him. I responded, "Judy, being represented as a gay man by a bunch of drag queens is like you being represented as a straight woman by a bunch of strippers." It took lots of conversations with Joel, and years of attending Gay Pride Parades for me to reconcile my feelings and feel good about the diversity in our community. Several years, after much processing as a family, we marched in the Gay Dads section of the parade with our sons.

When our first son left home, Joel and I were heart-broken, empty, useless and lost. Every moment of the last ten years had been dedicated to caring for him. Now he was gone from the house, the car, dining room table, and the refrigerator. We found ourselves riding in the car, just the two of us, with nothing to talk about. For ten years our every word was almost always about our son. What would we concern ourselves with, if not him? How would we plan our weekends if it didn't include his plans? How would the evenings be spent and what TV shows would we watch if they did not include his choices? These were painful months that morphed into years. Eventually we began to find the two individuals who had once been just two individuals. We discovered, again, that we could make noise when we had sex. We could spend Saturdays and Sundays that did not include a lunch at Chuck E. Cheese with other screaming teenagers or go to an adult movie that had actors in it that we recognized. We didn't have to buy massive amounts of stuff-your-mouth food and gallons of milk. We did not have to fill our freezer full of pizza for our son and ALL his friends. I found I was not replacing broken lamps and glassware every week. And, suddenly, we had a spare bedroom for guests.

So, why then, after an interval of nearly 14 years, did we decide to re-enter the trenches of parenthood? Good question! We have been asking ourselves that question for the past seven years. As much as we love our second son, we are still wondering what synapse snapped in our brains that gave the "O.K." to a second adoption.

Joel, as I said, had been involved in Gay Activism for many years. It was his passion and his avocation. We both felt that we had some good years left in us and that we both wanted to make one more, big contribution to support Gay youth. I dragged my feet for a long time. I was still exhausted from our first parenting experience. My career was peaking and my time was limited. I felt old and too out of it to relate to a child, much less a teen-ager, which is the only way we would be able to know that we were adopting a child who knew he/she was gay. Would we adopt a gay boy or a lesbian? How old would we want the child to be? It would mean selling our house in the gated, adults-only community in the city and moving to a family-friendly environment, again. We would have to re-learn all that multi-lingual talk and blend, once again, for the sake of the child. We talked and argued and anguished and finally the green light came on for both of us: we wanted to adopt a gay son. This time we had our parameters: no mental disability issues (Aspergers, Downs, Autism,) no one who would harm animals or set fires, no physical disabilities, and no one under fourteen. We wanted to be liberated again when this child reached eighteen.

Well, as the saying goes, "...the best plans of mice and men..." We searched and worked with our adoption agency and waited and waited for two years. I was TWO years older than I ever thought I would be for this project. Joel and I were just about to give up when we got THE phone call. They thought they had found just the right boy. He was thirteen, not fourteen, he loved animals, was not mentally disabled, had all his arms and legs, didn't set fires, and, best of all, he told his case worker that he was pretty sure he was gay. Voila!

111

The two years prior to taking our second son into our home turned out to be the easiest time. The hard work began when he arrived. We picked him up from his foster home, where he had been living for nearly two years. He had been inappropriately placed there. It was a special placement center for delinquent/troubled boys. Our son had been labeled a 'problem' because he was gay. He did not know this, and had acclimated to his surrounds quite comfortably. He learned how to hide anything that he didn't want stolen or broken. He learned to barter for favors and treats from the foster parents, in deference to the other boys who treated the adults poorly. He found a hiding spot in the woods where he could ride his bike and hide out from any violence or police action that happened to be churning at the house. He hated riding the Special Education bus to school, wearing the same clothes he had slept in the night before out of fear and worry. On the ride home back to our house, he cried all the way, grieving the loss of one of the most stable places he had been in ten years.

When a child is moved through twenty different foster homes in ten years, there are inevitable scars. Both of our adopted sons endured this abuse, but our second son was most affected. His trust level, especially of men, was zero. He hoarded food to his bedroom, not knowing when and if he would get another meal. He buried candy, fried chicken, gum, bread and cookies in his sheets, just in case… Having never had nice clothes, he did not know how to take care of them or what to do when they needed cleaning. Not unusual for children of his background, he was a bed-wetter till he was nearly 15. He was not forthcoming with information about anything he thought might get him in trouble or displease the adults. So, consequently, if we did not check his bed every day, he would continue to sleep, day after day, on urine soaked sheets. Of course, we insisted he take a shower every morning and wear clean clothes to school. Not used to taking showers regularly, he did not know that you put the shower curtain on the INside of the stall. Regularly, we had floods of water running out of the bathroom into the hallway until he got the hang of it.

No one had ever cared if he succeeded in school. Therefore, school was meaningless to our son. He had never connected with anyone except rare friends and one counselor in particular. Homework was out of the question. Living with two educators, one being an attorney-turned- teacher, the other a Middle School Principal, was a startling challenge for him. Joel and I are quite certain that if Joel had not been a teacher in the high school in which our son was enrolled, and if I had not been on the School Board, he would never have graduated. Of course, he will never admit that.

When he was sixteen, after many attempts to pass the driver's test, he got his license. Within a year and a half, he had crashed three cars, racked up multiple tickets, and lost his license. In the middle of his senior year, he moved into a friend's home and would occasionally come home to visit, ask for money or food, and disappear again for a while. He made an attempt to attend the local Junior College, failed all his courses, lost his loan money and drifted for about a year searching for employment. He has always had a penchant for choosing the other troubled kids as friends. They led him down the path to drugs and apathy. If we could get his attention, he would be very sweet to us and express his gratitude and appreciation for our efforts to help him. Most of the time, he wanted to be free of any adult intervention, since adults were the ones that had messed up his life in the first place.

Incrementally, almost imperceptibly, he started to come around. He began to listen and allow us to guide him and once in a while, he would admit that we had been right about this or that all along. At the end of a ten day cruise on the Seine River from Le Havre to Paris – a graduation gift for him – our son came up to the deck where we were sitting, starring up at the Eiffel Tower. He thanked us for the gift of the trip to Europe and for everything we had ever done for him. Of course, after he took off into the Paris night with other friends, we burst into tears.

There is no romance in adopting a child. There is no fairytale, happily ever after. The older the child is that you adopt, the more your heart will be broken. Guaranteed! "The Courtship of Eddie's Father" was a made-for-TV fantasy from the 1970's. In real life, Mrs. Livingston would have had the money stolen out of her purse, her credit cards would have been used to the thousands of dollars and her house would have been robbed. The Bill Bixby character would have been wrongly accused by the child of abuse and hauled off to jail while his home was ransacked by Eddie and all his friends.

Everything would have been sold off for drugs and food and Eddie would have landed in prison. Adoptive parents need to be prepared for anything.

The experience with our second son made the experience we went through with our first son look like a Sunday school picnic. He was not a bad child – quite the opposite: he was sweet and kindly and sensitive, always championing the under-dog. He was the victim of ten years of abuse and neglect. Our job was to endure, be resilient and forgiving, and hold on to the values that we knew were right for him. Joel and I had many, many discussions (arguments) as to what to do. Joel was very hard-line; I was a softy, I'll admit it. This caused major conflict in our relationship with each other and with our son. If you think you are going to be a 'perfect' parent, think again. There is no such animal! All parents make mistakes, over and over again.

Do I regret parenting two adopted sons? No! Would I do things differently if I had it to do over again? Definitely yes! Do I feel we created a functional family? Yes! I believe all families function in some form or other. Perhaps the term, 'dysfunction' is a word created from the perspective of the far end of a standard set in idealism. All families are dysfunctional from time to time. All families function, more or less successfully. The question is who survives? To what degree has survival prepared the family members for other family constructs in which they will find themselves? And, what becomes of those who do not emerge from family experiences intact? Is there an antidote?

If there is no vaccine or cure for damage endured from 'familyism', there is at least the hope of healing. If our society can put aside religious bigotry, economic prejudice and classist judgementalism, then we can begin to calmly explore diverse definitions of 'family'. We can have a conversation where all the members can come to the table and ask for what they need. We can begin listening then embracing change.

I used to tell my students who lived in an affluent suburban school district, "Just because something is different does not mean it is bad. It is just different". One of my employees who I had enjoyed getting to know and had taken an interest in his violent, deprived upbringing, came over to visit with his wife and two adorable infants. They were poor. He and his wife had never experienced anything but crushing poverty. When I took their babies in my arms, and looked into their blue, innocent eyes, a prescient aura came over me, and I whispered to them, "Good luck". At the end of that evening's visit, the young man and his wife took our hands and thanked us for the dinner and treats for their kids and said, "We have just never known anyone like you".

Today, Joel and I find ourselves the classic empty nesters. We see our boys when they want to see us or need something; we plan special events to snare them back into the family embrace, but not with the smothering dutifulness that we endured in our first families. We do not impose our values, our needs or our approval on them. They share most everything with us, sometimes to our dismay. But, we never let on that we fear for them or want to rescue them. We worry about them silently, at home, with each other. If we even have the slightest tinge to our tone of voice that says to them that we want to give them some unsolicited advice, they let us know that it is unwanted, and we stop.

So, to this day, we are still a changing family. The dynamic will always be surrounded in love. After all, love is all there is. Once we get past anger, fear, resentment and frustration, we emerge into acceptance, forgiveness, reconciliation and love. Sometimes I feel almost all of these emotions every day. Joel and I are fortunate that we have each other to process these feelings. We have always been good communicators. I have great compassion for single parents who work so hard to hold their families together, not having a partner with which to vent and make decisions. There was recently a CNN poll that reported that the American public is more sympathetic and accepting of Gay Families, than single parent families. This is unfortunate and an indicator of how much farther we have to travel down the road of understanding and accep-tance. It is not that Gay Families deserve more acceptance, but single parent families also need to be included in the em-brace of KIN. Anyone, gay or straight, who holds a family together in their loving embrace, is heroic and remarkable.

Where is it all going? What more can we expect from the changing family dynamic? The key is in the concept of CHANGE. Change is inevitable, as loathsome as it is for many people. The older we are, the more likely we are to dis-like things that change. The universe is changing, our little sphere that we call "World" is changing every day. Our bodies change and our minds and souls grow and change. It is inevitable that the families we grow up in and choose and reject and redefine and re establish will change. Dynamic, rather than static, makes us move forward. We move toward the future, not the past. We anticipate children and grandchildren, partners, spouses, and those beyond.

In 1985, before I moved to England, Joel and I went through the Quaker process of celebrating our commitment to each other. We spent months talking with clearness committees, answering questions and moving in to the LIGHT. Our celebration, on the 22nd of June, 1985, was attended by our first families and all our extended families. We, and about 200 guests, signed our names to this statement:

> **WE COMMIT OURSELVES** to live in an intimate sharing of concern, issues, monetary possessions and the space needed to provide mutual support with tender and watchful access to each other's needs.

> **WE COMMIT OUR TIME** to give and take an equal exchange of comfort, sexual energy, understanding and a healthy presence of mind, body, and spirit.

> **WE COMMIT OUR PRESENT AND FUTURE** trust to have exclusive sexual love, accommodating growth, change and newness as each perceives and experiences it.

WE COMMIT TO BEAR WITH the pain and fear that life will bring, avoiding rash judgments by trusting each other above anyone else and never denying ourselves anything that is communion.

WE COMMIT TO ALWAYS BE TRUTHFUL. If at any time we wish to change any of the terms of these commitments, we will do so only after seasoned consensus.

Finally, at the end of our Ceremony of Commitment, we sang the traditional Quaker song that brings everything and everyone full circle:

'Tis a gift to be simple, 'tis a gift to be free, 'tis a gift to come down where you ought to be, and when we find ourselves in the place just right, we will be in the valley of love and delight. When true simplicity is gained, to bow and to bend we shall not be ashamed. To turn, turn will be our delight, 'till by turning, turning we come round right. 'Tis a gift to be loved and that love to return, 'tis a gift to be taught and a richer gift to learn, and when we expect of others what we try to live each day, then we'll all live together and we'll all learn to say: 'Tis a gift to have friends and a true friend to be, 'tis a gift to think of others not to only think of "me", and when we hear what others really think and really feel, then we'll all live together with a love that is real. When true simplicity is gained, to bow and to bend we shall not be ashamed. To turn, turn will be our delight, 'till by turning, turning we come round right.

SOMETHING TO THINK ABOUT

Family Center

Family Friendly

Family restaurant

Family Grocer

Family Banking

Family Medicine

Family Practice

Family Fun

Family Counseling

Family Pharmacy

Family Van

Family Pets

Family Discounts

Family Mortuary

Family Values

Family Bargains

Family Swim

Family Pack

Family Car

Family Package

Family Rate

Family Prayer

Family Vacation

Family Tree

Family Ties

Family Room

Family Home

Family Estate

Family Fortune

Family Farm

Family Night	Family Business
Family Boarding	Family Heirlooms
Family Dental Care	Family Bible
Family Auto Plan	Family Jewels
Family Insurance	Family Camp
Family Recipes	Family Secrets